MIMESIS
INTERNATIONAL

MUSIC

N. 5

Stefano Marino and Eleonora Guzzi

THE PHILOSOPHY OF RADIOHEAD
Music, Technology, Soul

MIMESIS
INTERNATIONAL

Revised edition, translated into English, of the book *La filosofia dei Radiohead. Musica, tecnica, anima*, Mimesis, Milano-Udine 2021.
English translation by Dallas Hopkins, in collaboration with Stefano Marino

© 2024 – Mimesis International
www.mimesisinternational.com
e-mail: info@mimesisinternational.com

Book series: *Music*, n. 5
isbn 9788869774829

© MIM Edizioni Srl
P.I. C.F. 02419370305

CONTENTS

Stefano Marino dedicates this book to his son Marco, who despite his young age has already understood very well that "Music is the best".

Eleonora Guzzi dedicates this book to Lorenzo, thanking him for introducing her to the songs that over the years have become cornerstones of her life.

INTRODUCTION

1.

The title and subtitle of this book, *The Philosophy of Radiohead: Music, Technology, Soul*, were chosen to make the particular nature of this work, and the specific approach that we have adopted, immediately clear to our readers. Indeed, unlike many other works on Radiohead that have focused on the band's history,[1] the biographies of its five members (Thom Yorke, Jonny Greenwood, Ed O'Brien, Colin Greenwood, Philip Selway),[2] the reproduction (with comments) of the lyrics of Radiohead's songs,[3] or specific aspects of one of their albums in particular,[4] this work has a different aim: namely, the aim to offer an overall reconstruction and interpretation of what one might call the aesthetics of Radiohead, using an approach that can be defined, as the title suggests, «philosophical.» More precisely, this book certainly does *not* aim to hastily and arbitrarily present Thom Yorke as a philosopher in the canonical or strictly academic sense of the term, *nor* present the entire catalogue of Radiohead's work, from *Pablo Honey* (1993) to *A Moon Shaped Pool* (2016), as if it contained a philosophical doctrine or even a philosophical system. None of this, of course. Rather, the challenge and, if you wish, the ambition of this volume – in a manner similar, though not entirely identical, to other previously published works dealing with the connection between philosophy and pop-rock music[5] – is demonstrating that it is possible

---

1   See Randall 2011.
2   See, for example, Castelli 2022.
3   See, for instance, Franchi 2009.
4   Specifically dedicated to an analysis of *Kid A*, for example, are the books authored by Marvin Lin (2018) and Steven Hyden (2021).
5   See, for instance, Ferdori and Marino 2013; Marino 2014; Marino and Schembari 2021. In this context, it is also noteworthy to mention book

to establish a relationship between the world of philosophy and that of pop-rock music, one that is dynamic, rigorous, constructive and potentially enriching for both sides.

From this point of view, *The Philosophy of Radiohead* offers a focused interpretation of the musical production of this band in light of certain philosophical themes and questions, showing how this interpretive approach can reveal original meanings and stimulating implications. At the same time, this book also aims to highlight how certain philosophical themes and questions, in a way that may be unexpected or even surprising at first glance, can benefit from an interaction with a famous and successful product of pop-rock music (and thus of popular culture) from our times, like Radiohead's music, thus opening a potential reconsideration or even transformation of those themes and questions. Naturally, certain albums and, more specifically, certain songs will receive a privileged treatment here, that is, they will be selected and analyzed with greater attention and viewed as particularly paradigmatic examples of the aforementioned claims. For this reason, as we said above, this book has no intention to offer a complete analysis of Radiohead's whole discography, the history of the band or the group's entire musical trajectory. In doing so – as happens in more or less every interpretation of a cultural product, be it a poem, a literary work like a fiction novel, a philosophical text, a musical composition, a film, and so on –, a particular and precise approach was followed, concisely expressed in the three concepts that make up the subtitle of our book: music, technology, soul.

In our view, indeed, if it is possible to identify some aspects or elements that have made Radiohead's work truly unique – not only in purely musical terms, but also in terms of the cultural and even philosophical stimuli that this band's oeuvre is able to offer –, these aspects or elements should be understood first and foremost in the original and distinctive manner with which Radiohead has been able to articulate, reconfigure and manifest the relationship between music and technology (and, by extension, between technology and society) in its songs. However, we also posit that,

---

series like Open Court's «Popular Culture and Philosophy,» or Blackwell's «Philosophy and Pop Culture,» which often include, among others, also books on philosophy and pop-rock music.

in the case of a band like Radiohead, this *never* occurred at the expense of an essential expressive component that, in the subtitle of our book, we chose to condense and metaphorically express with a simple but undoubtedly evocative, emphatic and ambitious word: soul. Therefore, it is through the conceptual triad of «music, technology, soul» that we have taken on the task of deciphering what we call «the philosophy of Radiohead,» that is to say, the philosophical insights and meanings that, in various ways, are intrinsic to the music of this band.

Apropos of this, we would like to emphasize again that we make no claims of presenting an exhaustive and all-encompassing investigation, or an approach that aims to be unequivocal and «absolute» in its systematic nature. At the same time, however, we also believe that the readers of this book will find here a fitting and adequate interpretation of the musical oeuvre of Radiohead, undoubtedly one of the most important pop-rock bands of the last decades. In view of an investigation of the potential philosophical suggestions and implications that can be found in various moments of the gradual development of Radiohead's aesthetics (with specific attention paid to the aforementioned conceptual triad formed by music, technology and soul), in the chapters that follow we will show how the course charted by Radiohead can be placed alongside some observations on the relationship between art, technology and society, like those offered by a wide array of thinkers that may include, among others, Martin Heidegger, Max Horkheimer, Günter Anders, Hannah Arendt, Arnold Gehlen, and others. As our readers will see, especially the dialectical thought of Theodor W. Adorno (a German thinker who worked and indeed excelled in different fields: philosophy, sociology, musicology) has played an important role in the general orientation of our approach to the aesthetics of pop-rock music, exemplified here through the unique case of Radiohead.

2.

In an attempt to concisely present the fundamental aspects of our book and its basic structure, it is undoubtedly fitting to start with the main theme of *The Philosophy of Radiohead*. Therefore, we can begin by asserting that, on the basis of the interpretation that will be gradually developed in the four chapters of this book, the question concerning technology must be understood as the primary influence that conditioned, and perhaps even determined, the universe of sounds, words and images of Radiohead (what one could also call the band's «philosophy»). According to our interpretive approach, it is above all technology that shaped the creative languages and stylistic approaches adopted by Radiohead over the years. To be more precise, the real question at issue here is *not* merely the theme of technology in itself, but also (and more importantly) the presentation of what we may define the latter's inherently twofold or, so to speak, antinomical character.

Indeed, the English band, mostly starting with its third and groundbreaking album *OK Computer* (1997), has first confronted technology and then entered its depths in its following recordings, showing its ability to perceive, assimilate, incorporate and ultimately develop the intrinsic duality of technology in original and sophisticated ways. On the one hand, the music of Radiohead appears to be focused on the clear manifestation of a harsh criticism of a certain type of materialistic society that apparently operates in the name of technology, alongside a one-sided idea of progress that is unilaterally associated with it. From this point of view, the specific character of Radiohead's songs also appears to be focused on the need to express a strong desire to escape from a reality that is ultimately perceived as alienating and dehumanizing. On the other hand, however, starting with *OK Computer* and even more so in the following albums *Kid A* (2000) and *Amnesiac* (2001), Radiohead's music has found new motivations, original sources of inspiration and unmistakable creative impulses in technology itself. In our view, Radiohead has tried to identify a way to escape from our current technology-ruled world, characterized by sad and powerful dehumanizing tendencies (at least in some of its best known aspects and features), in order to arrive at a different and deeper poetic inner world that is nonetheless highly technologized but, although not entirely reconciled, attempts anyway to rescue the component of human expressiveness and restore the human being to its position as protagonist and, in a certain sense, leading figure of history, rather than subordinating the human being to the sheer power of a sort of technological determinism.

As has been noted, in the case of Radiohead this is less in the service of glorifying «the joy to live or the existential release when faced with the void,» but rather «the ability to continue to describe the void in an attempt to fill it, although only slightly and never definitively, with experimentation.[6]» Therefore, from this perspective, technology – often understood (or, better yet, perceived) by individuals as an alienating, destabilizing and often suffocating force –, if properly assimilated and mastered, reveals itself to be simultaneously a force that is able to gift new languages and original possibilities of expression to the human being that are better suited to, and efficient in, describing the existential malaise of our time and the discontents of our civilization. In our view, it is precisely this dialectics that makes the «philosophy of Radiohead» so fascinating.

An episode described at the beginning of Steven Hyden's book dedicated to *Kid A* can help exemplify this affirmation. The story is from 2019 (a year before the beginning of the Covid-19 pandemic, making Hyden's considerations even more sinister and revealing), when Thom Yorke appeared as a guest on the US talk show *The Late Show with Stephen Colbert*. The interview starts with the following exchange between the host and Yorke: «"For decades you've been writing music that is *uneasy* and *anxious* with regards to *society*, our government, *technology*, the general direction of the world," Colbert says, carefully setting up his punch line. "How does it feel to be right?" The audience bursts into applause. Thom chuckles, but it's one of those chuckles where you laugh because it's *true*, not because it's funny.[7]» After having shared this anecdote, Hyden continues the introduction to his analysis of Radiohead's *Kid A* that is developed throughout the book, observing:

> When you live inside a *future dystopia*, you can't really stop and comment on the *omnipresent bleakness*. When «bleak» is right *there*, it is no longer bleak. The *fear* is so near that you can't even see it. It is just ... normal. [...] *Kid A*, love it or hate it, was very much *a product of its moment*. It was *the definitive musical statement* about how it felt to live at the start of an *uncertain* new era, right after the

---

6 Alfieri 2019, p. 71.
7 Hyden 2021, p. 2 (emphasis added).

end of an old *fraught* one. In that way, it was tied to the cinema of the time. Movies like *The Matrix*, *Fight Club*, and *Vanilla Sky* arrived between 1999 and 2001, and were infused with deep *apprehension* about *modernity* and how *technology* disconnected people from one another, as well as a core essence of themselves. [...] *Kid A* signified a *cultural turning point*. Even if you didn't get the *how* of *Kid A*, you intuitively understood the *why*. It was a *confusing* album for a deeply *confused* time. [...] A *forward-thinking* work that at some point stopped being about the *future* as it gradually came to strongly evoke everything *vital* and *terrifying* and *unknowable* about *now*.[8]

As a pop-rock band that composed, recorded and played music at the turn of the new millennium, Radiohead chose to explore the depths of the universe of technology in a time that was particularly rich with important technological changes that would condition our everyday lives in an irreversible manner – if we simply consider the widespread use of the internet, as well as other innovations in communication like the invention of smartphones and a series of other devices that would influence our very way of being in the world, as well as the channels we use to experience and consume music. In other words, at the end of the 1990s Radiohead chose to adventure into a sort of undefined reality, one that was (and, in part, still is) unknown and heterogeneous, in which preconceptions and excitements, ghosts and fanaticism often mix, overlap and collide, fueling the enigmatic and fragmentary character of the present age. According to the interpretive approach adopted in the present book, Radiohead did this with the goal of coming into contact with such a dimension in the most realistic and immediate way possible, but simultaneously also in the most intimate and artistic way possible, by immersing itself, almost abandoning itself entirely, in the universe of technology. As some of Radiohead's most famous albums show, this turned out to be, in its essence, an adventurous musical experiment, clearly testified, for example, by the innovative and original methods of composition that the band fully adopted.

Such an exploration of the world of technology was possible for the band only after a radical change in its creative approach and a veritable revolution in its previous and well-established approach

---

8   Hyden 2021, pp. 2, 4-7 (emphasis added).

to composition, recording and performance. Radiohead chose to fully and unhesitatingly immerse itself in a dimension at times obscure and foreign, and therefore to expose itself to the risk of finding salvation (in the case of success) or condemnation (in the case of failure) in technology, precisely in a historical moment in which technology seemed to demand the subordination of humans, making the human being an object of its domination. In choosing to do so for rigorous artistic reasons (that may also have significant philosophical implications, as we will show), Radiohead experienced an unprecedented turn and a new definition to its career, thus renewing its musical language via a breakthrough that, due to its truly radical nature, has few precedents in the recent history of pop-rock music.

It is no coincidence that, for this reason specifically, Radiohead has arrived to be considered one of the most important bands of the recent decades and perhaps even *the* band that, overall, has been able to interpret in the most direct and radical way the uncertainties, conflicts and changes of human existence in the contemporary age. In this context, it can be useful, for example, to briefly introduce a comparison between Radiohead and Pearl Jam. As is well known, Pearl Jam is another band from the early 1990s that, much like Radiohead, has been able to «survive» until today – unlike many other musical bands from the same period that were swallowed (so to speak) by the vortex of contradictions and self-destructive tendencies that, as we know, are a part of the history of pop-rock music, often with tragic endings.[9] Beside this, it can be noted that Pearl Jam's musical production can also be understood as rich, in various ways, with philosophical suggestions, stimuli and contents.[10] However, unlike Radiohead, Pearl Jam apparently did *not* have in its decades-long career a truly radical and experimental «turning point» in terms of composition, recording and performance. Indeed, as Hyden notes:

---

9   As noted by Alfieri (2019, p. 25), «the triumph of Pearl Jam and Radiohead» is that of «long-lived bands that saw multiple decades and challenged the abyss of self-destruction which caused them to approach the present in different ways.»

10   On the «philosophy of Pearl Jam,» see the essays collected in Marino and Schembari 2021.

Pearl Jam really is an easy point of comparison here. [...] Pearl Jam never put out an album after the 1990s that stands apart definitively from the band's «classic» period. This is not meant as a knock against late-period PJ efforts like *Backspacer* or *Lightning Bolt* – it's just a fact that those albums didn't have the cultural impact of *Vs.* or *Vitalogy*. But *Kid A* mattered at least as much in Radiohead's career as *Pablo Honey*, possibly more. And then Radiohead put out another landmark LP, *In Rainbows*, seven years after *Kid A*, ensuring that Millennials would have their own Radiohead album as crucial as *The Bends* and *OK Computer* were for Gen-Xers. It's possible those same Millennials like *No Code*. But the relative conciseness of Pearl Jam's «relevant» era consigns them to '90s-band status, whereas Radiohead found a way, starting with *Kid A*, to be extragenerational.[11]

3.

As is well known, the concept of art is deeply connected to that of technology even from an etymological point of view and, therefore, in terms of both its conceptual and its actual history. In fact, «in Greek *téchne* is the word that lexically includes the family of meanings closest to the Latin *ars*,» so that, «in the oldest phase of the European languages, *téchne*, *ars* and their derivatives generally referred to any human activity implying certain capacities apt for a well ordered know-how.[12]» From this point of view, it can be useful to underline how it was art that over time continued to preserve and offer a reserve of creativity, expression and meaning, even during certain moments of modern and contemporary history in which the economically, socially and politically dominant technologies appeared pervasive, overwhelming and sometimes suffocating. Conversely, it is perhaps music, more so than other arts, that is able to reveal the insuppressible, structural and indeed constitutive relationship between art and technology. This relationship has always played an important role, up to the point that, in the attempt to «understand the nature of Western music through a historically constant principle,» some musicologists have identified «a pair of dialectically opposite poles, guided

---

11   Hyden 2021, p. 44.
12   Velotti 2005, p. 17.

by an inextinguishable inclination to synthesis,» in the concepts of «technology and emotion,» or more precisely «*mathesis* and emotion,» in which

> the term *mathesis* must be understood according to its original meaning of theory, science, knowledge [...]. Therefore, on the one hand, the freedom of emotion, an uninterrupted flow of a spirituality reluctant to extroversion but, at the same time, animated by the need to expand, to extend itself into intimacy; on the other hand, the research and testing of auditory combinations, technological design.[13]

In the case of Radiohead, we can say that the relationship of this band with the question of technology has been deep, constant and foundational, inasmuch as it has shaped its unique style over the years and has consequently defined the different results that Radiohead has achieved in the music scene from the 1990s until today. At the same time, it is also important to notice that this relationship has always been one in constant evolution. Indeed, a retrospective view of the full discography of the band, starting with its last album *A Moon Shaped Pool* all the way to its debut album *Pablo Honey*, makes it possible to identify a sort of multifaceted itinerary or development in Radiohead's career, following a *fil rouge* precisely represented by the evolution and transformation of the band's relationship with technology – in view of a broad meaning of this term, that encompasses both musical technique, in the strict sense of the word, and technology understood as a predominant factor of control and domination over the world that ultimately arrives to condition, or even structure, the current social, economic and political processes.

As we said, this is the specific interpretive approach that we chose to adopt in this book to try to decipher the «philosophy of Radiohead.» As happens with any interpretation, with our work we aim to disclose original perspectives on the phenomenon that is taken into close examination (in this case, the musical production of a pop-rock band), just like we aim to offer a new understanding of certain features and aspects that are present within the phenomenon and that truly define its essence. At the same time, it

---

13   Vizzardelli 2007, pp. 114-115.

is important to emphasize that we do *not* claim to possess *the* one and only correct interpretive approach and, therefore, that we do *not* aim to offer a final or definitive interpretation that may lead to exclude or eclipse other possible interpretations of Radiohead's musical oeuvre.[14] Neither absolute or entirely objective, nor arbitrary or merely subjective, the art of interpretation, due to its very nature, always lies in a delicate balance and somehow oscillates between different yet equally fundamental components, like stringency, methodological rigor and reasonableness, on the one hand, and imagination, enthusiasm and fancy, on the other. In methodologically presenting our concept of interpretation, we endorse Adorno's conception, according to which, in comparison to other disciplines, what is distinctive of philosophy is that it perceives even «the first finding which it lights upon as a sign that needs unriddling,» so that, for Adorno, the very idea of philosophy «is interpretation,» and precisely in this consists

---

14   From this point of view, it can be important to inform our readers that our book, *The Philosophy of Radiohead: Music, Technology, Soul*, is *not* the first work that attempts to develop a philosophical interpretation of Radiohead's musical oeuvre. In fact, to our knowledge, there is at least one other philosophical text on Radiohead in existence, namely the 2009 *Radiohead and Philosophy: Fitter, Happier, More Deductive*, edited by Brandon Forbes and George Reisch. We consider Forbes and Reisch's volume an important and instructive contribution to the same topic that we aim to investigate with this work. As our readers will see, *Radiohead and Philosophy* was one of the many sources cited in our book. Some chapters of this text were particularly useful because of the original perspectives they offered on certain aspects of Radiohead's music. At the same time, however, we believe that *The Philosophy of Radiohead* represents a project of a different nature: one that is characterized by some features that clearly differentiate it from a book like *Radiohead and Philosophy*. This is primarily in reference to the difference between an authored research monograph, like the present book, and an edited collection of essays authored by different authors, with a variety of topics approached from different points of view in each chapter, like Forbes and Reisch's co-edited volume. Secondly, although strictly connected to the first point, *The Philosophy of Radiohead* makes use of a precise, coherent and unifying interpretive approach entirely focused on three leading concepts (music, technology, soul) that, in our view, are able to guide us through our exploration of the main philosophical dimensions and implications present in Radiohead's fascinating musical adventures.

the great, perhaps the everlasting paradox: philosophy persistently and with the claim of truth, must proceed interpretively without ever possessing a sure key to interpretation; nothing more is given to it than fleeting, disappearing traces within the riddle figures of that which exists and their astonishing entwinings.[15]

4.

In the four chapters that articulate the structure of the present book we will take into account the aforementioned aspects and many others, investigating them in greater detail and examining the musical path of Radiohead by dividing it into three phases that, although connected to each other, nonetheless correspond to three different moments of the band's career. More precisely, these three phases or stages represent, in our view, three different ways to understand, unpack and elaborate the question of the relationship between the realm of technology, on the one hand, and the inner world of human expressiveness (or the «soul»), on the other.

According to our scheme and interpretive approach, the first stage coincides with the band's early awareness of the problem of technology that characterized its first albums, *The Bends* and *OK Computer*. Our readers, at this point, might immediately notice that we have just mentioned the band's second album, *The Bends*, rather than their debut album, *Pablo Honey*, as the starting point of our investigation. This is in no way a questioning of the quality of the songs in Radiohead's first album, as *Pablo Honey* undoubtedly includes several valuable compositions – among them one of the band's most widely recognizable and indeed legendary songs, namely «Creep,» a new version of which was released by Thom Yorke in 2021. Rather, our choice to assume *The Bends* as the starting point of our inquiry into the philosophical implications and resonances of Radiohead's music depends on the fact that *Pablo Honey*, if viewed retrospectively, has a vastly different style that «does not do fully justice to what Radiohead would have become a few years later.[16]» In short, differently than *OK*

---

15   Adorno 1977a, p. 126.
16   Solventi 2018, p. 42.

Computer, *Kid A* and the rest of Radiohead's musical oeuvre, an album like *Pablo Honey* is not concerned with «"art" or "experimentation" or "challenging music" [...]. *Pablo Honey* lacks mystery and ambiguity,» so that «[m]uch of Radiohead's career can be even interpreted as an attempt to bury its platinum-selling debut.[17]» As has been noted:

> *Pablo Honey*, the band's debut album, unmistakably arose from a rock lineage. It was released in February 1993, a couple of years after Nirvana's unexpected success [...]. The marketing savvy indelibly penetrated consumer consciousness when the word «alternative» itself was co-opted as a style of music. (Commodify your dissent, indeed.) Awkwardly but perhaps appropriately, Radiohead were swept into this narrative with «Creep,» a track that became an anthem for the disenchanted Gen Xers [...]. Radiohead were even touted as the «British Nirvana.» [...] But when *The Bends* dropped in 1995, no one knew quite what to do with it. [...] *The Bends'* influences were harder to identify [and] songs like «Planet Telex» and «My Iron Lung» not only rendered the Britpop tag useless, but also hinted at Radiohead's proclivity toward experimentation.[18]

Now, despite the wide gap that undoubtedly separates and differentiates *The Bends* and *OK Computer* from various points of view, it is nonetheless evident how in both albums, especially in regards to the themes and contents of many of their most representative songs, technology appears mostly as a sort of external enemy, i.e., as a threat both to the individual and society as a whole. Furthermore, it seems equally evident how such a conception of technology is presented by Radiohead to its listeners through textual and musical means that, on the one hand, are surely characterized by a certain degree of originality (especially in the case of *OK Computer*), but on the other hand are still quite traditional in their approach to composition, recording, instrumentation, etc. More precisely, we can say that, when listening to an album like *OK Computer*, various moments and passages already seem to hint at a sort of transition towards what we consider the second and more experimental stage of the aesthetics

---

17   Hyden 2021, pp. 45-47.
18   Lin 2018, pp. 59-61.

of Radiohead. However, at the same time it is also notable that a large part of Radiohead's legendary 1997 album seems to rest on quite usual expressive methods, musical materials and lyrical styles, which can still be categorized within the dimension of pop-rock music in a more or less traditional sense. From this point of view, in our book we suggest considering *OK Computer* as a transitional album, unlike *The Bends* that, despite its undeniable musical value, is a more conventional and, so to speak, mainstream work. From the first transitional moment, represented by *OK Computer*, Radiohead's meaningful stylistic change has gradually unfurled. This is perhaps one of the reasons why *OK Computer* is still considered today by many fans as the most important and emblematic work in the band's entire oeuvre, also because it represents Radiohead's first album almost exclusively based, as far as its concept is concerned, on questions related to the presence of new technologies in our lives.

In what we consider the first phase of Radiohead's complex relationship with technology, the latter is presented and narrated in the songs through voices, sounds and expressive modes that are not musically unusual or unfamiliar. In this phase a critical relationship with the real – including the role played by technology in society – is mainly expressed by Radiohead through the topics and contents discussed in the lyrics of the songs included in the first albums. It cannot be denied that the progressive development of technology also offers noteworthy advantages to humans: as such, technology represents an inevitable point of attraction (not excluding the fact that it simultaneously symbolizes, as part of the inextricable dialectics between two opposite poles, a threat and a risk). In any case, the world depicted in the lyrics of *OK Computer* is mainly built on alarming dystopian backdrops, unsettling descriptions proffered by disorienting figures that are rich with references to science fiction. At the same time, however, the musical instruments and tones used in *OK Computer*, and Radiohead's general compositional approach in this first phase of the band's musical path, are still rather traditional and may be defined as «analog,» rather than «digital.» Therefore, also in *OK Computer*, as in *The Bends*, the question concerning technology primarily involves the contents (i.e., the lyrics) of the songs, rather than the strictly musical dimension of Radiohead's work.

Moving to the second phase, we can say that we consider it a sort of intermediate moment, characterized by increased levels of complexity, hermeticism and at times «inaccessible» languages used by the band. From this point of view, this intermediate moment (which must be considered as absolutely central in the band's career) actually represents the period in which Radiohead was most committed to experimentation, which makes it a delicate phase that is emblematic of the band's musical development, since it marked the band's style in an almost irreversible manner.[19] This stage corresponds to the moment in which the members of Radiohead decided to fully explore technology (or, if one adopts the opposite perspective, allowed themselves to be fully absorbed by technology) and dared to probe the depths of technology to understand its logic and experience its most extreme consequences. Therefore, for Radiohead, this was the phase of a total immersion in the dark wilderness of technology, which is to say, more literally, the depths of an electronic and digital world that was still largely unknown, in order to truly discover it and identify both its potentialities and its limits, thus entering into contact with forms of expression that were original and at the time still unexplored, articulated by logics and systems that appeared fascinating and overwhelming at the same time.

In the band's musical journey, this second phase involved not only a radical experimentation in terms of sound (daring, digitalized, integral), but also, more generally, a new approach to compositional and creative methods. A stylistic innovation springs forth from this experimentation: an innovation that is undoubtedly evident to every listener, even at the first listening experience, a quivering creativity that finds its inspirational force in the depths of technology. The albums that strictly belong to this second phase, according to our interpretation, are *Kid A* and *Amnesiac*. As a consequence, in this period of the evolution of Radiohead technology appears as the undisputed protagonist, perhaps even the voice or the primary creative source from which the songs of these two albums spring forth, as if they were creations of technology. In

---

19   On this topic, see, for example, the analyses offered by Letts (2010), that are mainly focused on the developments that occurred during the period that spans from *OK Computer* to *Kid A* and *Amnesiac*.

other words, in the case of works like *Kid A* and *Amnesiac* technology appears as a sort of generator of the songs, as a voice through which the musical and emotional mood of the band is entirely filtered and digitalized. On this level, technology does not influence only the contents, and therefore the literary themes, of the songs, but also (if not especially), the structure and the extremely dense sound texture of the songs, which create a sort of integration and fusion between content and form that is admirable and indeed of a rare intensity. Synthetic, reiterated sounds, digital samples and unconventional computer procedures: each element in the aesthetics of *Kid A* and *Amnesiac* apparently comes from the future, emphasizing the detachment from the musical features that had characterized Radiohead's early work with unparalleled force. Once again, the imaginary universes that appear in Radiohead's songs are dark, undefined, quite often creepy and gloomy.

The third and final phase of Radiohead's trajectory, in our interpretation, represents a moment of synthesis and what one might consider the resolution of the conflicting and at times hostile relationship between expressiveness and technology that had previously emerged at various levels. However, it is important to note that this in no way distances Radiohead from the dimension that had been achieved in the second phase of its aesthetic development, in which this dimension had been reached through a radical rethinking of the band's own identity that somehow also implied a form of self-criticism. Rather, what characterizes the third phase of Radiohead's artistic path, in our view, is the capacity to establish a different relationship with technology, thus achieving a perspective that one might view as characterized by an explicit maturity. Indeed, in this final phase, technology certainly remains a fundamental element in Radiohead's songs, an essential part of the style of the band and, in a certain sense, a distinctive quality of its sound. At the same time, however, technology no longer seems to impose its presence in an absolute manner. In other words, adopting here a specific philosophical terminology (using the conceptual pair of «means/ends») to understand certain characteristics of this final phase that, as such, are purely musical, technology is no longer the end or goal that the band's compositions aim to reach, but it rather appears as the means used by the human beings to gain access to new creative languages and expressive possibilities.

Never before as in this phase had the intrinsic duality that defines the antinomical character of technology been so evident (which is also what lies behind its ability to fascinate, so much so that it can at times distract from the risks it conceals): in other words, the fact that both positive and negative aspects coexist in technology. In the albums *Hail to the Thief, In Rainbows, The King of Limbs* and *A Moon Shaped Pool* the electronic and synthetic sound of Radiohead undoubtedly continues to shape obscure and unsettling universes, destabilizing soundscapes that are not easily decipherable. At the same time, this electronic and synthetic sound also offers new and unparalleled modes of communication that allow the band to express the malaise of the individual in the contemporary age in the most extant manner possible. In this phase, technology seems to have made a band like Radiohead master of its own destiny, sure of the results of its creativity, in which technology is now an integrated stylistic element that has been reconciled with some of the features of the band's early aesthetics. In short, Radiohead appears now as a pop-rock band that holds a firm mastery of technology. So, the albums that we have chosen to include in the third phase of the evolution of Radiohead reintroduce the themes of the individual's precarious and unstable identity, and also of the individual's constant struggle to face the problems of a technocratic society.

If viewed from this philosophical perspective, the third phase of the evolution of Radiohead's aesthetics appears to be characterized by a sort of rediscovery of the centrality of the human being as the focal point (or, so to speak, the barycenter) around which the band rebuilds the narrative of its musical discourse. As we said, in the previous phases this narrative had rather challenged the sometimes radical outcomes of fragmentation and even desolation deriving from an excessive presence of technology in our world, grounding this critical confrontation with technology on an intrinsic need of consistency and autonomy. Furthermore, what happens in the third phase of Radiohead's musical work is in no way in contrast with the fact that this phase is also one characterized by a strong social and political component, in terms of a critique of the deformations and even obsessions that can derive from an unscrupulous and unreasonable use of technology in our highly technologized, digitalized and also globalized world.

Indeed, the human dimension, the «constant representative of a heart wrenching and melancholic vision,» continues to play a special role in Radiohead's work and is especially reflected by «Yorke's melodies and the harmonic sensibility of many elements of the arrangements[20]» of the band's songs. In this context, it is no coincidence that the songs on Radiohead albums like *Hail to the Thief*, *In Rainbows*, *The King of Limbs* and *A Moon Shaped Pool*, notwithstanding their complexity, are more singable, if compared to many of the songs belonging to the previous phase. Furthermore, the songs included in Radiohead's last albums seem to feature a vital return of traditional and analog musical instruments (although still accompanied by digital instruments as well), and also of more familiar, canonical sounds that are characterized by a more human and «people-oriented» dimension.

5.

In the four chapters of this book we will examine and bring to light some of the most significant themes that can be found in Radiohead's songs, with a constant focus on the difficult relationship between technology and soul (two keywords from the subtitle of our book), as the linchpin of our interpretation. The analysis of the songs we have selected in the following chapters is precisely oriented towards the three-phase scheme that we have briefly explained so far, although not rigidly, but rather flexibly (as is always required, in our view, in the case of interpretations of artistic phenomena). Summarizing, the «philosophy of Radiohead» that we present here to our readers is based first and foremost on a strong emphasis of the twofold and complex nature of technology: an aspect, the latter, that has found a reflection not only in various contexts of contemporary philosophical debates, but also (in terms of the specific subject of this book) in Radiohead's music, describing the evolution the band has undergone since its adoption of technology first as a theme of the contents of the songs' lyrics and later as an approach to composition and a musical resource at every level. From a certain point of view, we can say that

---

20   Alfieri 2019, p. 75.

the band's relationship with technology was characterized at first by diffidence and fear that, however, over time has resulted in a situation of inspiration and complicity.

On this basis, the first chapter of *The Philosophy of Radiohead*, starting with some songs from the first period of the development of the band's aesthetics, will attempt to analyze the condition of contemporary individuals in light of their relationship with technology: a condition that, in short, can be summarized with concepts such as alienation, domination and reification. Indeed, based on what seems to emerge from some songs that are particularly emblematic of Radiohead's early work, in a strongly technologized world like the current one individuals increasingly tend to alienate themselves from society, losing contact with reality as they become confused by the various virtual realities and media dimensions that they simultaneously participate in. The result of this process is a sense of isolation from the community, a withdrawal into oneself which is often accompanied by a suffering over one's (real or supposed) shortcomings, causing the individual to search for an ideal and imaginary escape. In this condition of alienation, estrangement and detachment, the subjects seem to struggle to understand the meaning of what they do and the importance of concrete actions, and furthermore seem to live in a totally artificial, altered and unnatural time dimension. This condition, in the case of our investigation of the «philosophy of Radiohead,» can be especially associated with the first phase of the band's stylistic evolution: namely, the phase in which technology is understood primarily in the songs of Radiohead as a sort of new and unexpected adversary that risks to suffocate basic human needs. This causes the negative aspects of technology to be more noticeable in this phase, compared to its positive aspects.

In the second chapter, our investigation focuses on the relationship between technology, society and culture, with several references to Horkheimer and Adorno's concept of the cultural industry (first introduced, as is well known, in their seminal philosophical work *Dialectic of Enlightenment* from the 1940s). In this chapter, above all, we will attempt to offer an analysis of the way in which the electronic and digital dimension belongs to all of the band's songs in the second phase of its creative evolution, imposing itself in every fragment and moment of the artistic process, not unlike how technology increasingly takes on the shape of a virtual network that silently surrounds human beings and gradually conditions every aspect of life in contemporary society. This chapter, which coincides with the aforementioned second phase of Radiohead's career, dialectically overturns the entirely negative perspective on technology that had previously emerged, thus leading to a greater attention toward the positive side of the twofold and contradictory nature of technology. In this chapter, we will thus examine how Radiohead's daring experimentation with new technologies at a strictly musical level strongly characterized the (definitively revolutionized) style of groundbreaking albums such as *Kid A* and *Amnesiac*. This brings to light how technology itself provided components, stimuli and innovative resources for the creation of a new musical language and a new aesthetics that is no less critical of contemporary society, compared to the style of the first phase of Radiohead's evolution.

Lastly, the third chapter, which corresponds to what we consider the third phase of Radiohead's complex and fascinating evolution, draws attention to the last period of the relationship between Radiohead's music and technology, which apparently evolves towards a sort of integration and conciliation of the opposed terms involved in this relationship – whereas the fourth and final chapter of the book is of course dedicated to Radiohead, but with a wider perspective that involves not only pop-rock music but also, as we will see, jazz and 20th-century avant-garde music. At this point, the music of the band seems to rediscover what we may define the personal, intimate and expressive dimension of human experience, as testified by some of the themes that characterize the songs of the albums belonging to the third phase. However, at the same time, the band's musical style, despite the partial reappearance of more canonical arrangements and traditional instrumentation, still bears traces of the spark of technological experimentation, as well as traces of the previous phase, in which the search for a unique sound that passed through the universe of technology had irreversibly determined the band's creative potentialities. Indeed, precisely through a radical use of technologic and digital experimentation (and *not* despite or against it) Radiohead was able to regain control, in a moment of transition in which the band had apparently risked to losing it. So, in its final phase of development, the band has reshaped its musical language, in order to take back a more instinctive, spontaneous, almost youthful awareness that had been partially lost in the previous phase. This awareness is also underpinned by a lucid and disillusioned perspective that has allowed the band to instill a fascinating and dynamic dialectics between the opposite poles of enchantment and disenchantment, naivety and skepticism, in many songs included in Radiohead's last albums.

In light of this, even personal and introspective reflections, much like the component primarily oriented towards a critique of society, seem to acquire a greater efficacy and perspicuity. The voice of the first-person narrator in the lyrics of many songs belonging to this third phase is often that of the contemporary individual who is by now aware of being unable to entirely evade the net and logic of technology that shape the world in the present age. It is precisely with this awareness (and by making use of these technological resources) that the narrator incessantly sings of his distress, of taking on new forms and nuances, and carving out vital spaces within an artificial-technological environment. This corresponds with a new form of indirect and mediated emancipation that passes through technology itself, rather than manifesting itself in a more direct and immediate manner through a mere contraposition.

The themes that can be found in the lyrics of the songs included in *Hail to the Thief*, *In Rainbows*, *The King of Limbs* and *A Moon Shaped Pool* are undoubtedly heterogeneous and varied in their contents. However, according to our interpretation, each song at least in part reflects themes such as the subject's troubles, difficulties and uncertainties in the present, the difficulty of human relationships in a digitalized and virtual world, the need for a greater closeness to and protection of nature, and so on. The impact of the idea of a mediated and indirect union, not free from problems, between the human being and technology often appears (and resonates) in these songs as strong, intense, deep, primordial and visceral. Further proof of this resonance can be seen in the solo album entitled *Anima* that Thom Yorke released in 2019, which is focused on the feeling of anxiety and worry that afflicts the individuals and grips their souls, validating more than ever the idea of a creative process and a narrative characterized by a sense of technological dystopia and, at the same time, by the desire to openly confront the challenge that technology represents, rather than flee from it.[21] In conclusion, in the interpretation that we offer in *The Philosophy of Radiohead*, technology, understood in its complexity and its disorienting power in the contemporary age, hovers, twists and reclaims its place in Radiohead's entire musical catalogue, although in ways that differ from album to album, thus representing the keystone of the entire aesthetics of one of the most emblematic and representative pop-rock bands of our time.[22]

---

21   From this point of view, it might be intriguing to try to extend the interpretive approach adopted here apropos of Radiohead also to the investigation of some important side-projects of the various members of the band, such as, for example, Thom Yorke's membership in Atoms for Peace and The Smile. However, such an extension of our investigation would go far beyond the specific and delimited scopes of a book like *The Philosophy of Radiohead*, so that it will eventually become the object of potential future publications.

22   The present book represents a revised version, translated into English, of our book *La filosofia dei Radiohead*, originally published in Italian in 2021. The English translation of our text, realized by Dallas Hopkins, was financially supported by the University of Bologna, which we would like to sincerely thank for this opportunity. All lyrics of Radiohead songs quoted in this book are cited directly from the versions available in the official catalogue of Radiohead albums published as a book under the title *Radiohead Complete* (2017).

CHAPTER ONE
THE INNER WORLD OF THE INDIVIDUAL
The Bends, OK Computer

1.

In the first part of «Paranoid Android» (certainly one of the most famous, meaningful and iconic songs ever released by Radiohead), a human voice that sounds at times robotic whispers «I may be paranoid, but not an android» below Thom Yorke's restless singing, almost as if, despite it all, the difficulties, worries and fears were what make the human beings what they are: imperfect, fragile, vulnerable, fallible creatures, which in turn makes them also unpredictable beings. More concisely, something quite different from a machine – in spite of all the comparisons, that are nowadays (in)famously common and frequent, between the human way of thinking and experiencing the world, on the one hand, and computers, algorithms and Artificial Intelligences, on the other.

In this chapter, as we had already explained in the Introduction, we will analyze what we consider the first phase of the relationship between music, technology and soul in the aesthetics of Radiohead: in short, we will focus on the particular role that technology played in the band's unique imaginary, starting with its early albums, *The Bends* and *OK Computer*.[1] These two albums, from our perspective, can be both seen as works belonging to the initial phase of the band's artistic journey, not simply because they chronologically represent the foundation of Radiohead's discography, but also because they constitute the starting point of a creative journey that laid the foundations and established the presuppositions for the subsequent development of the band's distinctive

---

1   The underlying reasons for our choice to exclude from our philosophical investigation Radiohead's first album, *Pablo Honey* (1993), were already discussed in the Introduction. For a general comment about the songs of *Pablo Honey*, see Doheny 2002, pp. 8-29; Franchi 2009, pp. 22-75.

style. We nonetheless find it necessary to add that a recording like *OK Computer*, according to the interpretive approach adopted in this book, could also be included in a sort of intermediate or transitional phase in the band's career. Indeed, this album is marked by a rupture in the relationship with the traditional motifs previously used by Radiohead, but seems likewise characterized by a style and creative approach that is still too canonical, so to speak, to be considered entirely experimental and therefore be placed entirely within the second phase of the band's style, as we defined it in the Introduction. Radiohead's artistic transformation starts precisely with *OK Computer* and is nothing but the natural and essential growth and development of the intrinsic aesthetics of the band, according to a conception in which the relationship between the inner world of the individual and technology becomes progressively more central, with all of the purely artistic changes dictated by new technological developments (alongside those happening at a sociopolitical level).[2]

As we have already underlined in the Introduction, technology has largely influenced the musical language and style of the band beginning with a fundamental characteristic, which is to say the dualism that technology entails and brings along with it in every context: a dualism represented by the fact that technology may constantly and simultaneously embody both positive and negative aspects for the human beings. This intrinsic duality – the same feature that makes technology a point of attraction and fascinating element for humans, on the one hand, while also representing something obscure with ambiguous, dark and even dangerous fringes, on the other – can be succinctly represented by the line (and the imaginary that it evokes) «an airbag saved my life,[3]» which appears in «Airbag,» the opening track of *OK Computer*, almost as a sort of mission statement. The meaning of this song is quite easy to intuit: Thom Yorke is clearly speaking about cars, in a sort of futuristic, space-age context, and the danger that these modern, sophisticated creations may pose to humans, despite the

---

2   For an original interpretation of *OK Computer* that understands it as symptomatic of «the death of the classic rock album,» see Footman 2007 (in particular, pp. 41-123).

3   Radiohead 2017, p. 88.

fact they have become indispensable elements of daily life. In fact, during some public appearances Yorke has never concealed his fear of means of transport and the dangers they may pose on the road, due to the lack of full control that humans have over vehicles.[4] Nevertheless, for the specific purposes of our interpretation the relevance of this statement mainly lies in the fact that technology (symbolized here by a car) can represent both a threat and salvation. In this sense, the airbag of a car is the perfect allegory of this dualism: «In a fast German car, I'm amazed that I survived, an airbag saved my life.[5]»

2.

Starting with their second album, *The Bends*, Radiohead had already begun to consider the remarkable presence of technology in our society: a presence that, given the existential problems of the individuals and constantly remaining in their shadow, would slowly and imposingly extend its influence to the entire musical language used by the band.[6] «Street Spirit (Fade Out),» the last track of *The Bends*, like a submissive, disenchanted prayer, recognizes the fleetingness of human life and encourages distancing oneself from machines, as the latter would further isolate the human beings from their inner world, and poetically urges the listeners to «immerse [their] soul in love[7]» through a «brief, luminous

---

4   «Thom had been in a car crash just after sitting his final school exams and [...] had been wary of cars and transportation in general ever since. As Thom explained to *Time Out*: "Nothing scares me more than driving [...]. I hate it because it's the most dangerous thing you do in your life". [...] Thom takes this obsession one stage further in the lyric to "Airbag," where a transportation crash becomes a redeeming, almost Christ-like experience» (Doheny 2002, p. 60).

5   Radiohead 2017, p. 88. Based on this image, we also find it interesting how technology may represent safety and salvation, but specifically regarding dangers that it exposes us to: if one never drives or rides in a car, then the airbag is superfluous. We owe this observation to Dallas Hopkins, the translator of the English edition of our book, whom we would like to thank.

6   For a general comment about the songs of *The Bends*, see Doheny 2002, pp. 30-55; Franchi 2009, pp. 78-135.

7   Radiohead 2017, p. 63.

and almost liberating ascension in the finale.[8]» A song like «Street Spirit (Fade Out)» rests entirely on a chord progression of lyrical, painful and aching arpeggios that are repeated over and over. Only the chorus, with its incessant, disillusioned lines «And fade / Out again, / And fade out[9]» discloses an intense and moving melodic development that can be compared to a crack letting in a ray of light rather than an aperture. However, the chorus does not alter the song's fundamental meaning, but rather enhances, through this fleeting contrast, its crude realism: the human being is finite and is self-conscious of his/her mortality (which, following Heidegger's *Being and Time*, ontologically defines the *Dasein*'s unique way of «being into the world[10]»), unlike machines that are unable to conceive of this sense of finitude.

«Fake Plastic Trees,» the fourth track of *The Bends*, is a rather traditional ballad – and this is perhaps one of the reasons behind it being one of the band's most famous hits, as well as being a fan favorite – based on a progression of four chords and a regular 4/4 musical meter. Despite the song's popularity and apparent simplicity at a structural and musical level, its lyrics deal with decidedly deep and topical questions, like society's obsessive tendency towards consumerism facilitated by new technologies. By saying this, we aim to make reference to an actual situation of worship of material objects that each of us has probably experienced at least once in our lives, in a sort of vicious circle in which the market supplies astronomically increases at, and has an incessant need to be fueled by, a demand that, for its part, often appears to be induced by the artificial creation of unnecessary needs. This vicious circle becomes particularly visible in the case of fetishization processes and in the actual obsession with consumption and the acquisition of new industrial products, as they are thought of as bringing wellness and happiness. In this context, the fear of remaining outdated in terms of the latest trends encourages continuous and compulsive purchases, reinforced in turn by the recent advent of online shopping.

---

8   Solventi 2018, p. 79.
9   Radiohead 2017, p. 62.
10   Heidegger 1996, §§ 12-13, pp. 49-62.

As a result of this behavior, what we can often observe is a divergence between genuine needs and merely perceived ones, between actual realities and merely artificial ones, where the latter are understood as mere creations resulting from the abstract logic of the market. The individual, operating as buyer and supposed «master,» by virtue of his/her presumed freedom of choice, is ultimately revealed to be a sort of «slave» to the market and a «victim» of the culture industry.[11] Overwhelmed by the abundance of goods of every type and variety, and subject to the commodity fetishism and the primacy of exchange value over use value,[12] the individuals struggle to maintain control over their actions.

The question concerning technology (as discussed in the homonymous essay by Martin Heidegger[13]) has represented a veritable *topos* of contemporary thought, often intertwining philosophical concepts in the strict, rigorous sense with concepts from other disciplines in a fruitful and stimulating manner, involving subject areas like sociology, economy, anthropology, psychology or also the natural sciences. Critically analyzing the thoughts of authors like Günter Anders, among others, the Italian historian of political thinking Michela Nacci, in her book *Pensare la tecnica*, has presented this issue, stating that in the contemporary age «things dominate humans, an obsession with consumption abounds, and a profound spiritual misery prevails.[14]» Through this lens, human beings are portrayed as «primitively» and inextricably linked to their instruments – which is to say the objects they own, like «prepackaged goods and clothing[15]» – and as increasingly unable to trust in their more authentic, genuine and original abilities: «the speed of consumption has decidedly become "waste," the continuous generation of new desires.[16]»

Due to the speed of production and the parallel increase in consumption, intimately tied to the vicious circle discussed above, commodities deteriorate quickly and are replaced with increasing rapidity. It is no coincidence that today many products are

---

11   See Horkheimer and Adorno 2002, p. 113.
12   See Adorno 2001, pp. 37-39.
13   See Heidegger 1977.
14   Nacci 2000, p. 126.
15   Nacci 2000, p. 95.
16   Nacci 2000, p. 80.

designed, advertised and distributed on the market with planned obsolescence, giving merchandise a limited life span in order to facilitate their rapid replacement. Furthermore, the industrial system (and, consequently, also the consumers' preferences) has become almost totally standardized: the sprawling market aimed at the multitudes tends towards mass production based on an identical repetition, progressively abandoning attention to detail and originality, characteristics of a less homogenizing market, giving way only to what we might call, with Adorno, pseudo-individualized differences.[17] According to Jean Baudrillard (interestingly cited in a monograph on *Kid A*), «[w]e make believe that products are so differentiated and multiplied that they have become complex beings, and consequently purchasing and consumption must have the same value as any human relation.[18]» Alongside Adorno and Baudrillard, many other intellectuals of the 20th century claimed that the homogenization and unification imposed by machines, technologies and industrial processes (and nowadays algorithms and AI, we might add) have favored a uniformity in thought and, in particular, a deterioration and an impoverishment of our power of critical judgment. According to these and still other thinkers, this has generally rendered the human experience more approximate, superficial and unfree, i.e. lacking in terms of free, deliberate and critical evaluation.

The uniformation and unification of thought, and the fetishistic worship of the objects, have found fertile ground in the constant development of new technologies like radio, television, internet, social media, and so on.[19] A simple, banal world is depicted through the screens of our technological devices, a presentation that

---

17   On the concept of pseudo-individualization, applied to the processes that characterize the culture industry (and, in particular, popular music), see Adorno 2009, pp. 287-290.

18   Baudrillard, cited in Lin 2018, p. 47.

19   Interestingly, it seems that streaming services like Netflix have pushed television further towards what intellectuals like Baudrillard were suggesting in some of the works cited in this book: the plethora of choices available to us makes the experience of watching streamable content increasingly «personal,» and the ability to rewatch films and series can lead to the creation of pseudo-relationships with characters. We owe also this observation to Dallas Hopkins, the translator of the English edition of our book, whom we would like to thank.

Baudrillard would call a «simulacrum»: an immortalized image of a reality frozen by clichés and characterized by empty forms, in which «[t]he emptiest of feelings[20]» rule, to cite Radiohead's song «Let Down.» We are faced with complex mechanisms of which we are not always aware and that cannot be entirely examined here – as such a discussion would be too distant from the specific objectives of a book centered on the philosophical interpretation of a pop-rock band –, but that are nonetheless relevant in better understanding the vast system in which the late modern (or, as others have suggested, the postmodern, or even post-postmodern[21]) individuals participate, and also to enter more deeply in the poetic universe of Radiohead.

Returning now to «Fake Plastic Trees,» we can therefore say that this song seems to express to the listener the same bored, restless attitude of the individual in the contemporary age, in line with the attitude described by various Western thinkers that reflects an understanding of reality «solely comprising quick, incoherent and unscrupulous images that ultimately spill into boredom.[22]» The structure and instrumentation of the song is rather canonical: the traditional sound of a young pop-rock band from the mid 1990s, partly comparable to the so-called Britpop sound of those years. However, it is notable that the lyrics and the feelings of emptiness they exude are quite current, even today: it is a declaration and call to awareness of the fact that apparently there are no solid values to cling to, nor ideas or even methods to draw from, only useless, insignificant objects, mere ruins that attempt to fill the people's sense of emptiness. These objects do not actually represent or express anything, but fill our «plastic» lives that exist in a sort of «faceless» world, it too made of «plastic»: «Plastic People,» to cite here *en passant* the title of one of Frank Zappa's most iconic songs from the late 1960s that predicted certain phenomena destined to explode just a few years later.

«Fake Plastic Trees» is quite emblematic and illustrative of this specific phase of Radiohead's career. The song can be understood as an explicit declaration of a youthful malaise that was already

---

20   Radiohead 2017, p. 96.
21   See Michaud 2019, pp. 85-109.
22   Nacci 2000, p. 81.

expressed in post-punk movements of the 1980s and in the grunge scene of the early 1990s. As Alessandro Aflieri explains in his book *Rocksofia*: «Grunge bands responded to hyper-semiotization with a return to the essential. [...] The essential nature of their songs expressed this sense of dissatisfaction that belonged to an entire generation, far from both the political enthusiasm of the 1970s and the sense of party-loving communalism of the 1980s.[23]» In the mid 1990s, Radiohead confessed a lack of values with simplicity and honesty, and also with a certain sense of resignation and realism, aware of the fact that even feelings, an essential aspect of human life, had become fake, standardized, commodified and plastic-coated.

After the initial description of a sort of parallel world made of rubber and plastic, the lyrics of «Fake Plastic Trees» narrate the story of a girl: «She lives with a broken man, / A cracked polystyrene man / Who just crumbles and burns. / He used to do surgery / For girls in the eighties, but gravity always wins.[24]» The inadequacy and the hedonistic superficiality of an imaginary attributable to the 1980s return (and, in this regard, it is worth noting that just two years later another hit that is still quite recognizable today would ironically comment: «Life in plastic / It's fantastic![25]»), along with a reference to human relationships that are literally crumbling because they lack any sort of solid foundation or authenticity. After the song's climax and an increase in tension, Yorke desperately cries out: «She looks like the real thing / She tastes like the real thing / My fake plastic love.[26]» Here plastic becomes a metaphor for the materiality, emptiness and commodification that oppress the human beings in the present age. The nostalgia of what once was (or seemed to be) true, authentic and genuine, but no longer exists, proves to be more intense and almost paradoxical (or, at the very least, anachronistic), if compared to the context of complete artificiality that seems to have steamrolled the human being, according to this pessimistic vision of modernity.

---

23 Alfieri 2019, p. 32.
24 Radiohead 2017, p. 46.
25 This is quite obviously a critical reference to the Danish band Aqua and its song «Barbie Girl,» a summer hit from 1997.
26 Radiohead 2017, p. 47.

3.

A few years later, it is the protagonist of «No Surprises,» the tenth track of *OK Computer*, that will face the very same «wrong life» – an expression that evokes Adorno's well known concept in *Minima moralia*.[27] Much like «Fake Plastic Trees,» this song has a more or less traditional instrumentation, but the linear, bright harmonies are the background for a set of lyrics that are anything but soothing. The verses narrate the tormented mentality of a man that has passively resigned himself to an ordinary life; the chorus rhythmically and repetitively reminds the listener with a certain constancy «No alarms and no surprises,[28]» thus expressing the individuals' attempt to adapt to the conventions and habits of a society that are in some way forced upon them. It is as if outside of these established social norms there was nothing but isolation and frustration, a poor life far from the standardized luxury and fun («a job that slowly kills you, / Bruises that won't heal / You look so tired, unhappy[29]»). The protagonist of «No Surprises» lists what an ordinary man aspires to and the desires whose satisfaction would inspire this pseudo-happiness: material objects that offer nothing but an immediate sense of gratification, «[s]uch a pretty house and such a pretty

---

27   Indeed, it is this phrase that appears in one of the most famous and striking aphorisms in Adorno's *Minima moralia*: «Wrong life cannot be lived rightly (*Es gibt kein richtiges Leben im falschen*)» (Adorno 2005, § 18, p. 39). Many years later, in his 1963 lectures on the problems of moral philosophy, Adorno would affirm to have rediscovered a similar position on the «wrong life» in Nietzsche (see Adorno 1996, p. 1): in particular, in some observations that can be found in the aphorisms 33 and 34 of *Human, All Too Human*, where we read: «Every belief in the value and dignity of life rests on false thinking [...]. The great majority endure life without complaining overmuch; they *believe* in the value of existence, but they do so precisely because each of them exists for himself alone, refusing to step out of himself [...]: everything outside themselves they notice not at all or at most as a dim shadow. Thus for the ordinary, everyday man the value of life rests solely on the fact that he regards himself more highly than he does the world. [...] [M]ankind has as a whole *no* goal, and the individual man when he regards its total course cannot derive from it any support or comfort, but must be reduced to despair. [...]. The whole of human life is sunk deeply in untruth» (Nietzsche 1996, pp. 29-30).

28   Radiohead 2017, p. 104.

29   Radiohead 2017, p. 104.

garden.[30]» A connection can be drawn here between this line and «Fake Plastic Trees,» with its reference to a «fake Chinese rubber plant.[31]» The lyrics of «No Surprises,» dragged along by the painful affirmations of the protagonist, reveal a potential tragic ending: this ordinary man is on the verge of a crisis, a decline into the abyss of depression, when he realizes that his ordinary, sanctioned and prearranged life is actually inauthentic and offers no possibilities besides sinking into total apathy and emptiness («I'll take a quiet life, a handshake, some carbon monoxide[32]»).

According to the pessimistic perspectives developed by a large part of 20th-century philosophies of technology, the latter «does not entail violent repression,» but «exists because humans desire it, because technological objects are thought to improve our lives, making them more convenient and pleasant.[33]» Just like in many Radiohead's songs, no alarms and no surprises are desirable in routine, instead only objects that can make our daily lives more comfortable in some way. From this point of view, alienation (adopting here a broad, general definition of this complex philosophical concept), or what we might call the total acquiescence in the empty values of consumerism imposed by mass society, proves to be a singular choice that is the responsibility of the individual: a choice that is nonetheless difficult to truly make and, above all, difficult to fully and exclusively attribute to the individual alone, as it is influenced by a mindset that society, the economic system, and technology voluntarily or involuntarily impose on the individual himself/herself.

Radiohead's third studio album, *OK Computer*, offers numerous and evident examples of blame and criticism toward – as well as a recognition of – the power that new technologies hold over society, much more so if compared to the previous two albums.[34] What is expressed at the poetic and musical levels of Radiohead's work in this phase of the band's career seems to be connected to certain philosophical visions of a postmodern context, according to which the science and technology are «the driving forces» that

---

30   Radiohead 2017, p. 105.
31   Radiohead 2017, p. 46.
32   Radiohead 2017, p. 104.
33   Nacci 2000, p. 138.
34   For a general comment about the songs of *OK Computer*, see Doheny 2002, pp. 56-82; Franchi 2009, pp. 138-208.

dismantle «established certainties, [...] fragment the subjectivity, and de-realize (which is to say strip away the actuality of) the reality.[35]» In both contexts – the music of Radiohead and the more explicitly philosophical context of Western thought – the individual wanders around, confused, uncertain and alienated. The increasingly refined and functional technologies of modern society not only continue to impose their presence on the individual in every context and every moment of his/her daily life, from the workplace to home, from working hours to free time, but they also silently dictate the rhythms, expectations and norms of society as a whole. In turn, human beings attempt, often unconsciously, to adapt their habits and lifestyles to the rigorous, cold and calculating standards of technology, demanding of themselves and of others a level of efficiency that is increasingly difficult to achieve. Contemporary society asks us to be increasingly optimized, happier, more productive, to the point that one arrives at the foreboding realization that «to be human, [...] you must be inhuman, technological, artificial, or android,[36]» that is to say (to express this concept in a more straightforward manner) that to be truly accepted in society the individual has to operate like a computer, developing a sort of algorithmic thought process. Speed, efficiency, passivity, submission, indifference, rigidity, perfectionism: all these capacities and qualities are *not* fit for a promotion of human well-being and happiness, but are seemingly necessary today for receiving social recognition and success, and, when possible, achieving a sufficient level of self-esteem, «[o]therwise, all this universe offers is isolation and emptiness.[37]»

As we develop further, more general considerations based on some of the philosophical points of interest found in «No Surprises,» followed by the themes featured on the rest of *OK Computer*, the idea is that individuals of the contemporary epoch, discouraged by this comparison with the standards and norms imposed by technology, often feel unfit (or, to use a well known expression from Günter Anders, «obsolete» or «outdated») with regard to their social context. It is for this reason that contemporary

---

35   Nacci 2000, p. 184.
36   Fiorelli 2009, p. 123.
37   Fiorelli 2009, p. 123.

individuals often find it difficult to spontaneously trust in their own abilities, if not through attempting to adapt themselves to the logic imposed by machines, according to which the affirmation and integration of the self in the collective constitute indispensable moments in the «sane» and «healthy» development of the individual identity and personality. Therefore this comparison between humans and machines can easily create frustration, as machines impose performance criteria that are unfit for the human nature. In this sense, at times the individuals, upon self-reflection, encounter isolation and emptiness, perceiving themselves as different from the masses that seem to act automatically and function mechanically,[38] which results in the alienation and detachment of the individual. In this case, the sensation of being unable to perfectly fulfill the required duties and tasks, and the resulting fear of failure, judgment and exclusion, can easily create frustration, panic, confusion, and alienation. In some ways this is what happens to Marvin the Paranoid Android, one of the fictional characters in Douglas Adams' novel *The Hitchhiker's Guide to the Galaxy*, which inspired the homonymous song by Radiohead. Marvin is an atypical android with an eccentric human-like personality; indeed, he is misanthropic and melancholic, in a constant state of suffering and depression, tormented by doubts and uncertainties, which are all human characteristics. It is this same sense of uncontrolled torment that Thom Yorke expresses as the song «Paranoid Android» opens with the first verse, through a particularly effective and agonizing image, one that almost seems to suggest the paradoxical dreamlike associations that independently make their presence known during sleep: the lead singer describes the unnerving situation in which insomnia wins, in this case because of «all the unborn chicken voices in [his] head.[39]»

---

38   «In 20th-century philosophical thought there is an extremely strong connection between these terms: technology and masses. Indeed, the conceptual chain that goes from "the masses" to "mass civilization" all the way to "mass culture" has multiple points of contact with reflections on technology [...] [M]asses, crowds, they are the opposite of the rational, controlled individual. These concepts instead coincide with: hysteria, violence, uncontrolled emotions, unrestrained passion and irrationality, decreased reasoning abilities, lack of control» (Nacci 2000, p. 129).
39   Radiohead 2017, p. 89.

4.

Numerous intellectuals of the 20th century have severely criticized technology and depicted it as a sort of enemy of human thought and sensibility, understood as the most noble and unique components of the human being. As Michela Nacci notes,

> [t]hrough this lens, technology is the opposite of human practices, of the customs and habits that define the individuals or communities as specifically human: they are the practices through which stories, the past, memories, societies are all created, where we develop symbols that help us recognize ourselves as individuals and as groups.[40]

This opposition between artificial technologies, on the one hand, and human sensibility and thought (or «soul,» to use one of the concepts from the subtitle of this book), on the other hand, has clearly taken on various nuances in the works of different intellectuals that can be ascribed to the aforementioned constellation of contemporary philosophies of technology, drawing from a variety of theoretical, ethical, aesthetic or political perspectives. For example, in placing more or less emphasis on certain aspects of the human condition in the technological age, some intellectuals concentrated on the negative effects of technological developments that, for example, are primarily the result of the transition from slower forms of communication to faster and newer ones, considered as more immediate, instant and unfiltered, ultimately «hostile» to the complex, arduous construction of robust and reliable human relationships.[41] According to other thinkers, instead, the negative effects of the «bulimic» state of technology in our time are mainly the consequence of the recent transition from an attitude of genuine curiosity and even awe towards our surrounding reality to an attitude of disillusionment and disinterest, where the increasingly ease with which we use new technologies has gradually suppressed a genuine desire for knowledge and a sense of wonder towards the world. This posture could be seen as the

---

40 Nacci 2000, p. 62.
41 See Nacci 2000, p. 63.

opposite of a concept like «intellectual rationalization,[42]» which is the tendency to excessively rationalize every event through a techno-scientific lens, thus ignoring the «ancestral» human proclivity for mystery and spirituality. At the same time, this rigid, disillusioned attitude is also accompanied by a sense of infantilism, at times defined as a sort of «permanent puberty,[43]» which alludes to a condition in which human beings lead their lives as if they were children, detached from the consequences, meanings and ends of their actions, amusing themselves with technological devices (that often end up performing tasks in their place) in a state of unawareness, yet without truly understanding these devices and the effects they have on human existence.

As is well known, in the context of 20th-century philosophies of technology the critical theses presented by Günther Anders in his work *The Outdatedness of Human Beings* can be included among the most original, most radical and most influential contributions on this theme.[44] Anders underlines how the human beings, by their very nature, are incapable of adapting to the speed of machines and rapidly rationalize their thoughts, habits and behaviors according to the changes imposed by machines. According to this philosophical perspective, human beings are somehow «imperfect» (although it is precisely this «imperfection» that makes them unique), while technology is (or rather claims to be) «perfect»; human beings are incomplete and mortal, while technology today seems to claim completeness and a sort of infinity (for instance, in terms of a potential infinite development and progress, etc.); human beings cannot compete with the peculiar «immortality» that technology is seemingly able to bestow upon its products. In an attempt to imitate the machines, humans repudiate their nature, thus reducing themselves to a condition of «slaves» and developing feelings of shame. This is probably one of the roots of alienation, the sensation that apparently dominates society at present; and the present tends to already be considered the future, for the sake of speed, the constant updates, and the unceasing modification of productivity processes. For Anders, this

---

42   Nacci 2000, p. 71 (with specific reference to Weber).
43   Nacci 2000, p. 74 (with specific reference to Huizinga).
44   See Anders 1956.

disadvantaged position does not simply imply a loss of the sense of one's identity in the world, but also a loss of the world itself. Reality as such is gradually abolished, because our experience of reality becomes superfluous. Indeed, the world becomes a reflection mediated by technology (in the previous century through television and radio, while today primarily through the internet, social media, the power of algorithms, and ultimately the increasing potentialities of AI) that is presented to us as a simplified, standardized and commodified image of reality, one that is virtual rather than real. In other words, if viewed through this lens, technology threatens to sever our immediate and spontaneous contact with reality, removing the control human beings have over their own experience and work, transforming them into a cog within an enormous machine in which every action is pre-determined and individuals wander «simply among their [...] devices like disturbed prehistoric animals.[45]»

In this context, and connected to what we have stated thus far (despite the doubtless differences, from several points of view, between all these great philosophers of the 20th century), also some theses presented by Max Horkheimer in his work *Eclipse of Reason* can be of great relevance.[46] Horkheimer, for example, focuses on the gradual (and, for him, tragic) relegation of critical thought to the dimension of the inessential in our society. In the essentially and inexorably utilitarian «administered world» that we live in (to cite a well known expression coined by Horkheimer and Adorno in *Dialectic of Enlightenment*[47]), there seems to be a tendency to provide optimal material conditions for human existence (though certainly in asymmetrical and unequal ways across society), but at the price of the exclusion of everything that is considered purposeless, autonomous, genuinely critical of the existing social order and, above all, not easily marketable. What is missing from this frame is a space for critical reflection, and this absence is aimed at giving free reign to technological-industrial productions, economic interests, and the power of ruling groups. According to critical theorists like Horkheimer, this situation can be understood as

---

45   Nacci 2000, p. 90 (with specific reference to Anders).
46   See Horkheimer 2004, especially pp. 3-62.
47   Horkheimer and Adorno 2002, pp. XI-XII.

a manifestation of the paradoxical and contradictory «irrational rationality» of modern society: a society that assimilates, identifies and standardizes, which is quite visible in the fetishization processes and the obsessive consumption of entertainment commodities.[48] As Horkheimer critically observes in *Eclipse of Reason*:

> The human being, in the process of his emancipation, shares the fate of the rest of his world. Domination of nature involves domination of man. Each subject not only has to take part in the subjugation of external nature, human and nonhuman, but in order to do so must subjugate nature in himself. Domination becomes «internalized» for domination's sake. What is usually indicated as a goal – the happiness of the individual, health, and wealth – gains its significance exclusively from its functional potentiality. These terms designate favorable conditions for intellectual and material production. Therefore self-renunciation of the individual in industrialist society has no goal transcending industrialist society. Such abnegation brings about rationality with reference to means and irrationality with reference to human existence. Society and its institutions, no less than the individual himself, bear the mark of this discrepancy. Since the subjugation of nature, in and outside of man, goes on without a meaningful motive, nature is not really transcended or reconciled but merely repressed.[49]

Putting aside the points of interest in the critical reflections of the members of the Institute for Social Research that are generally associated to so-called Frankfurt critical theory (Horkheimer, Adorno, Marcuse, etc.), we can also take a look at certain topics discussed by Arnold Gehlen, one of the most eminent exponents of another leading tradition in 20th-century thinking, namely philosophical anthropology. Despite the enormous distance in terms of methodology and, above all, political ideology, between a conservative thinker like Gehlen and a Marxist critical theorist like Adorno, it is notable that the two developed a close, rich relationship in the 1960s, which brought to light certain convergences in the critical examination of what Adorno and Gehlen respectively called the «culture industry» and the «industrial

---

48   Nacci 2000, pp. 93-94 (with specific reference to Horkheimer).
49   Horkheimer 2004, p. 64.

culture» of our time.[50] In the context of the present investigation, it can be interesting to note Gehlen's use of the term «primitivism» to refer to the inclination of the masses to respond to external stimuli through uncontrolled reactions and a sort of «overstimulation of the senses,[51]» and therefore without the mediation of reflective, critical thought. According to a critical and openly pessimist view such as this (as well as being, in Gehlen's case, a view that is politically conservative and even reactionary, and hence clearly distant from the one of Marxist theorists like Adorno and Horkheimer), in the technological age individuals seem to show an increasing tendency to renounce their individuality and singularity, their personal and autonomous judgment, instead fully abandoning themselves to the conformism that is characteristic of mass society.

5.

After the short philosophical excursus developed in the previous section, let us return now to our main topic, i.e. the philosophical interpretation of Radiohead's music. Apropos of the concept of alienation, that we have briefly summarized and sketched here (and that we aim to apply to the interpretation of some Radiohead songs in the first phase of the band's career), we can say that, in the present context, we mostly tend to associate this concept to a condition of distancing, estrangement, denial, but also escape from reality in search of ideal, imaginary and fantastic worlds in which one can hope to establish his/her own personal order and hence regain the status of master of his/her own actions (or delude oneself into thinking this possible). The human being, still able to imagine new horizons and different scenarios, but at the same time unable to find fulfillment, authentic gratification or approval in the aseptic world of technology, attempts to move towards new destinations as a gesture of rebellion against society or in search of inner comfort: those who do not see themselves reflected in society, or fully realized in it, attempt to distance

---

50 On this topic, see Marino 2021a.
51 Nacci 2000, p. 94 (with specific reference to Gehlen).

themselves from it. This is apparently the scenario described in «Subterranean Homesick Alien,» the third track of *OK Computer*: a song whose title is clearly reminiscent of Bob Dylan's famous track «Subterranean Homesick Blues» (1965) and in which the narrator imagines being kidnapped by aliens, strange creatures that hover in the sky.

The narrator of «Subterranean Homesick Alien» describes life in a strange city whose inhabitants keep their spirits tightly locked away and live pained lives because of the secrets they keep. The narrator dreams of another world: «I wish that they'd swoop down in a country lane, / Late at night when I'm driving. / [...] / Take me on board their beautiful ship / Show me the world as I'd love to see it.[52]» As if from afar or on a screen, the narrator imagines observing human beings in their claustrophobic, frenetic lives, which helps him gain an awareness not of how the world *is* but how it *could* or *should be*. Beyond the specific meaning of «Subterranean Homesick Alien,» this reading can be interestingly compared to Adorno's negative-dialectical philosophy, whose conception of self-reflective and critical knowledge is, on the one hand, certainly aimed at grasping «what is,» but, on the other hand, does *not* consider this kind of knowledge as sufficient and rather favors the development of the capacity to also consider the existing social order «in light of what could be[53]»: that is, in light of the implicit and still unexpressed potential that is secretly present in the reality and that, if properly released and fully developed, could finally lead to a radical transformation of the society and a real improvement of human life. As Adorno claims in his important 1965 lecture course *Metaphysics. Concept and Problems*, «the task of philosophy is precisely to *understand*, and not simply to reflect, what happens to be»; then, Adorno connects this ambitious conception of the task of philosophy to the need to preserve «[t]he possibility of seeing through [the existing] situation as a context of guilt concealed through blinding, and thus of breaking through it.[54]» As Adorno explains to his students:

---

52   Radiohead 2017, p. 93.
53   Schweppenhäuser 2003, p. 44.
54   Adorno 2000, pp. 113-114.

the world in which we live arouses a kind of mistrust towards philosophy [...]. The fact is that the deeper philosophy grows and the further it is removed from the surface of the merely existent, the harder it becomes to free oneself of the feeling that, through its depth and remoteness from mere existence, philosophy is also growing remote from the way things really and actually are, *comment c'est*, as Beckett puts it. One has the feeling that the depth of philosophical reflection, which is necessary as a resistance to all the illusion with which reified consciousness surrounds us, at the same time leads away from the truth, since one sometimes suspects that this same existence which it is the inalienable impulse of philosophy to penetrate and go beyond, is the only thing which exists and is worth reflecting upon *at all*. [...] If the pedestrian replacement of knowledge by the mere registering, ordering and summarizing of facts were to have the last word against the elevation of thought, truth itself would really be a chimera, and there would be no truth, for truth would be no more than the practicable summarizing and arranging of the merely existent. The suspicion I am expressing here and which, I would say, is an indispensable *moment* of philosophical speculation, is that trivial, positivist awareness may today be closer to the *adaequatio rei atque intellectus* than sublime consciousness. I believe that the only way out of this dilemma would be to reflect on the idea of truth itself, and to grasp truth, not as an *adaequatio*, not as a mere measuring against factual circumstances, but as a procedure adopted towards a being of a quite different nature and dimension, and tied to a quite different procedure of consciousness than mere registration. [...] [O]ne will not survive by preserving some so-called higher spheres, or what I would prefer to call nature reserves, which reflection is not allowed to touch, but by pushing the process of de-mythologizing or enlightenment, to the extreme. Only in this, if at all, is there any hope that the philosopher, through his self-reflection, will not end by consummating triviality, the consummation of which is absolute horror.[55]

The suspended and somehow undefined atmosphere present in the lyrics of «Subterranean Homesick Alien» finds a perfect correspondence in the song's properly musical dimension, especially in its musical arrangement through a series of futuristic, eerie sounds in the background, produced by Jonny Greenwood's

---

[55] Adorno 2000, pp. 114-115.

guitar. In this case, much like in the rest of the album, the instrumentation is still rather traditional (electric guitars, bass, piano, drums), although the band is clearly oriented towards a musical experimentation that will be performed and made more explicit in the following phases of the development of Radiohead's aesthetics. The image of technology that paints it as superior to human beings – an image that is so intriguing because it can be read as both a source of salvation and as a threat to life on earth – continues to be a strong pole of attraction. At times, escape seems to be the only viable solution, an expression of the individual desire to distance oneself from a culture and history that cannot be changed and that are no longer shared. Of course, escape from reality does not necessarily entail an escape into a science fiction universe; it can simply mean a partial evasion of everyday norms, an attempt to avoid a predetermined destiny, a reawakening from a suffocating reality or also something like a personal, inner revolution.

This is the case of Radiohead's «Exit Music (For a Film),» the fourth track of *OK Computer*, a true anthem of escape, change, overturning of established rules, an intimate act of rebellion in the name of emotions and ideals that by now seem lost, outdated, purely romantic. «Wake from your sleep, the drying of your tears, / Today we escape, we escape[56]»: the song, composed for the film *Romeo + Juliet* directed by Baz Luhrmann, features lyrics that reference the titular characters who, in Thom Yorke's imagination, decide to overturn the laws dictated by their families and run away together. The sad, at times even depressing atmosphere, underpinned by a melancholy acoustic guitar, is subdued; Yorke's pained voice is complicit in this creation, «almost lugubrious, limply resting atop the solemn procession of the acoustic guitar,[57]» and the song oscillates between more unsettled and intense moments, moved by a romantic insurrection emphasized by the «arrival of the mellotron[58]» in the first chorus, and other more disheartened, despondent moments. Whether these forms of escape are real or purely spiritual and

---

56   Radiohead 2017, p. 94.
57   Solventi 2018, p. 118.
58   Solventi 2018, p. 118.

imagined, and whether the ultimate destination is earthly or divine, is unimportant here: what is paramount is the act of fleeing itself. As Thom Yorke confirmed in an interview: «the most important thing about music is the sense of escape it gives us.[59]» With his characteristic succinctness and discretion, Yorke seems to emphasize here the meaning behind the artistic creations of Radiohead in this phase of its career and the need of the members of the band to distance themselves from the ruling criteria of contemporary society, the same criteria that 20th-century humanist thought has challenged many times.

A final reflection that brings us to the conclusion of this chapter is related to a rather striking contemporary phenomenon that is tied to the changes induced by new technologies and the perception that modern human beings have of temporality compared to the past. Indeed, it is possible to suggest a comparison and differentiation between slowness and the cyclical nature of biological rhythms, on the one hand, and simultaneity and the speed of performance (and, above all, change) imposed by technology and progress, on the other hand. This rapidity is revealed by the ease of use of many machines and the increase in industrial production. In this frame, human beings tend to distance themselves from natural vital rhythms and this quite often creates tension, fatigue and alienation. Today, human life is articulated by the intense rhythm of machines and computers, so much so that even our perception of time and reality is often accelerated and altered.

Following Hannah Arendt, it can be argued that the advent of modernity caused the gradual disappearance of the primacy of the *vita contemplativa* (contemplative life) and the imposition of the model of *vita activa* – which, in turn, is articulated for Arendt in three kinds of activity: labor, work, action.[60] With this, the idea of «doing» or «making» was progressively dominated by the relation to manufacturing, production and consumption, more so than to «acting» in the truest sense of human agency.[61] In this regard, also the rather lucid and forward-thinking view from Georg Simmel

---

59   Yorke, cited in Draper 2004, p. 20.
60   See Arendt 1958.
61   Nacci 2000, p. 87 (with specific reference to Arendt).

in his short but dense 1903 essay *The Metropolis and Mental Life* comes to mind, more specifically his thoughts on the condition of hyper-stimulation and over-excitement experienced by the individuals living in the age of standardization, technification and intellectualization of life.[62] If we compare the passing of time to an inner subjective flow, a flow that is therefore impossible to reify, grasp or truly measure, it seems undeniable that today individuals live faster than in the past. How much time and care do even the simplest of daily experiences truly require (not to mention more complex activities, like artistic endeavors) to be fully «lived,» and how much time do we actually have available in our frenetic days to experience events and relationships in a way that cannot be reduced to mere distracted consumption?

«Hey man, slow down, slow down, / Idiot slow down, slow down[63]»: these words, taken from «The Tourist» (the closing track of *OK Computer*), sound like a warning, a contemplated admonishment that rises above the notes played by Jonny Greenwood on a slow, distended, captivating «triple time» that «makes it very difficult for the listener to get any sense of rhythm or orientation,» and that creates an atmosphere of «reverie,» a sensation of spinning «gently like a galaxy into the void.[64]» Yorke's lyrics seem to describe the distinctive pace of modernity: «They ask me where the hell I'm going? At 1000 feet per second,[65]» as if it was necessary to go ever faster, as if the time available was never enough, flashing before us in rapid frames, so fast that it is impossible to understand the meanings and connections of our actions, to the point that we are no longer able to understand what we think and what we do. Indeed, this song is a reference to the typical attitude of tourists (a key figure of our age of widespread «aestheticization,» characterized by the paradoxical «end of art» and the simultaneous triumph of beauty in everyday life[66]), that attempt to visit every single attraction as quickly as possible, without truly enjoying or experiencing the real beauty of natural landscapes

---

62   See Simmel 1997, pp. 174-185.
63   Radiohead 2017, p. 106.
64   Doheny 2002, p. 82.
65   Radiohead 2017, p. 106.
66   See Michaud 2019, pp. 49-60, 152-173.

or artworks, apparently suggesting how easy it is to live superficially when one lives so quickly, losing sight of things, actions and the rhythms of our bodies, which are ultimately the lens through which we perceive and experience the world.[67]

Music, including pop-rock songs, can help shatter this loss of critical consciousness or this «illusion» (that is paradoxically the result of an extreme «disillusionment» connected to the increasing scientificization and technification of our world), which is to say that it is perhaps through art, including music, that we can still bring our focus back to our lives and regain contact with what we may call the natural rhythms of human experience. Within the specific scope of this book, it is interesting to note how this can occur also entirely at the music level of a composition. Indeed, «[b]y chopping and slicing time in their music,» musicians like Radiohead «break us away from ordinary existence and its ordinary rhythms. They violate our temporal expectations and routine and force an awareness of time. They compel us to ask ourselves how we arrived at this particular place in our lives.[68]»

Through the particular poetic content of the lyrics, but also and above all through musical elements (like, for example, certain changes in musical meter and rhythm), it is possible to regain an awareness of temporality that the contemporary human being seems to have lost. From this point of view, if all of this strictly belongs to the realm of music (at the level of the technique employed in a specific composition, etc.), one can also legitimately imagine a return to life *through* technology, i.e. thanks to it and even by means of it. As we will see, this concept takes on further value and meanings that are much more ambitious and radical as Radiohead moves to the next phase of its fascinating aesthetic evolution.

---

67 In contemporary philosophical debates the central role of the body has been especially analyzed and emphasized, for example, by Richard Shusterman's somaesthetics, a new disciplinary proposal launched by Shusterman at the end of the 1990s and precisely dedicated to the philosophical investigation of the «ontological centrality» of the body «as the focal point from which our world and reciprocally ourselves are constructively projected,» beside other important «epistemological, ethical, and socio-political issues» connected to the body (Shusterman 2000, pp. 270-271).

68 Thompson 2009, p. 121.

CHAPTER TWO
THE DOMINION (AND DOMINATION) OF TECHNOLOGY
Kid A, Amnesiac

1.

As we have explained in the previous chapter, the atmosphere or mood of alienation that we sometimes find in Radiohead's songs is tied to the contemporary individual's difficulties in relating with, and integrating into, a world controlled and dominated by technology (and an extremely industrialized and administered socio-economic system, in association with technology). Put simply, it is a world in which a sort of natural selection – problematically applied also to the cultural and social world, in a socio-biological fashion – seems to be the only prevailing law; a world in which nowadays culture is inevitably intertwined with the market, whose profit-based logic is underpinned by, and fused with, continuous technological innovations, thus establishing also an interdependence between the market, art and technology.

These are all aspects that, with reference to some of the most important and at times pressing questions in the current aesthetic debates, can be also linked to certain issues related to what has been emphatically defined as the transition, in the last decades, to so-called «artistic capitalism.[1]» Of course, this aesthetic characterization of the nature of contemporary capitalism should *not* mislead us into imagining a world that has become unexpectedly marvelous and sublime – as suggested by Yves Michaud's thought-provoking observations, when he writes:

> It is incredible how beautiful the world is. Many things are beautiful, from products in their packaging, designer clothes with their stylized logos, muscular bodies, bodies that have been reshaped or rejuvenated through plastic surgery, faces embellished with make-up, or faces that have been retouched or smoothed, piercings and

---

1   On this topic, see for example Lipovetsky and Serroy 2016.

personalized tattoos, a protected and preserved environment, the spaces of our daily lives furnished with inventions from the world of design, cubic-futurist military equipment, uniforms with a ninja-like or constructivist style, combinations of food presented on plates decorated with artistic sketches – or more modestly packaged in multicolor bags in supermarkets, like Chupa Chups lollipops. Even dead bodies are beautiful – delicately wrapped in plastic covers and lined up at the foot of ambulances. If something is not beautiful, it is therefore necessary that it becomes so. Beauty reigns. In any case it has become an imperative: be beautiful, or at the very least, spare us your ugliness. I obviously write in jest: such beauty is in the eye of the beholder and these imperatives are in our minds. Beyond this, if one refrains from using these strictly aesthetic categories, what re-mains is the same ocean of ugliness (note that, despite this change, in this case beauty is still the category surreptitiously used), horror (so as to at least slightly change the categories), and the common drivel that characterizes our ordinary world. Simply change glasses and perspective to discover a world that is no longer beautiful or ugly, a world that should be understood through other qualities and dimensions, that unexpectedly returns to an older form, presenting itself the way it was able to in other times and cultures. [...] By now, however, the glasses of aesthetics are firmly placed on our nose and notions of beauty are deeply rooted in our heads. We, the civilized humans of the 21st century, live in the age of the triumph of aesthet-ics, a devotion to beauty, the age of its worship.[2]

In reality, on closer examination, if it is true that «[c]apitalism has turned aesthetic» today, this does *not* mean

that life under capitalism has necessarily become fulfilled, that it entails human flourishing, that labor has finally been organized «ac-cording to the laws of beauty.» Far from it! Rather, it has become «aesthetic» insofar as the production of value now draws heavily upon «creative industries,» on the labor of the «creative classes,» on aesthetic strategies of distinction and the modulation of affects. [...] Surplus value now springs from speculation in the realm of the «Spectacle» itself, and many contemporary marketing strategies widely appropriate classical aesthetic discourses.[3]

---

2   Michaud 2019, pp. 49-50.
3   Gandesha and Hartle 2017, p. X.

Turning our focus more specifically to music, from this lens and in this context, the relationship that musicians and bands establish with the culture industry is undoubtedly intricate, complex and contorted, but ultimately inevitable. As Alessandro Alfieri has noted, «the tension in rock music is the paradox of rock, in light of the fact that,» despite all the attempts at rebellion that have marked the history of rock music (even bestowing upon it a legendary status), «its birth and existence are inscribed anyway within popular culture and the culture industry.[4]» In other words, it is not unusual that musical styles, approaches and attitudes that are (or that at times simply appear so) innovative, transgressive or capable to express a form of dissidence and protest can be quickly «swallowed» and absorbed by the culture industry and the market. This ultimately reveals that these products belong to the market, thus confirming the culture industry's capacity to popularize what, at least at first look and in its deepest intentions, aims to embody a critique and even a negation of popular culture, at least in its mainstream forms. In certain aspects, this process can easily bring to mind the unflagging capacity of the fashion system to assimilate the subversive power of various phenomena of anti-fashion, such as trends deriving from so-called street style movements, ultimately replacing them over the years,[5] following the inexorable logic of fashion based on the «principle of the new» that merely aims to replace something old with something new that, in turn, will soon become old and be replaced with something else.[6] Apropos of this, fashion scholars sometimes tend to speak of «from-subculture-to-massculture» processes,[7] in order to express such a particular dynamic.

Now, according to our interpretation, the awareness of not being able to fully flee from the power of the culture industry and show business, and from the «internal dialectic tension» that characterizes rock as a musical genre – which ensures that «[e]ven when rock appears in opposition to the established order and the dominating commercial mindset, in reality [it] engenders a dialectical

---

4   Alfieri 2019, p. 8.
5   On this topic, see for example Chiais 2020.
6   See Svendsen 2006, pp. 9-35.
7   Kramer 2021, p. 139.

spiral[8]» of what it claims to be in opposition to –, has always been very clear to Radiohead. In fact, the band always turned a critical eye towards these aspects of pop-rock music and, at the same time, belonged to this genre, also sharing its conception of it with the listeners. In this sense, Radiohead's attempts to partially free itself from (or, from another perspective, to avoid fully adopting) the established rules of the culture industry and the market are well known, as well as the band's attempts to exploit these rules in its favor on some occasions. In this context, we would like to suggest to consider Robert Fripp's calm, stringent and rigorous idea of being «in the marketplace but not governed by the values of the marketplace[9]» – which is to say working *within* the music industry as a sort of *outsider*, as a «small, mobile, independent, intelligent unit,[10]» in search for a way out from the suffocating alternative between a strict adherence to a merely consumerist aesthetics, on the one hand, and artistic marginalization, on the other – as a sort of «golden rule» for every pop-rock musician wishing to establish an informed, active and, so to speak, self-conscious and reflective relation with the culture industry and the star system (rather than a passive and unreflective relation), in order to prevent falling prey to them.

2.

If the aforementioned maxim of Robert Fripp (the founder and leader of the legendary band King Crimson) can truly be adopted as a «golden rule» for all pop-rock musicians that, as we said,

---

8   Alfieri 2019, p. 9.
9   Fripp, cited in Tamm 1990, p. 92.
10   Fripp, cited in Tamm 1990, p. 89. As has been noted, «[o]n the level of the music industry,» in the mid 1970s Robert Fripp «had developed grave reservations: a dinosaur itself, "the rock & roll business is constructed on wholly false values, impermanent and mainly pernicious, although not in an obvious way." [...] Later, toward the end of the 1970s, Fripp would develop a systematic critique of music industry practices, write it up, and publish it in *Musician, Player, and Listener* magazine. For now he simply knew that he had had enough, and was looking to a future of "small, independent, mobile and intelligent units" to replace the lumbering Mesozoic automaton behemoths that passed for rock acts in 1974» (Tamm 1990, p. 66).

wish to establish a conscious, active and reflective relation with the culture industry, the market and the star system, then we can say that the members of Radiohead, in their own way, have also distinguished themselves in this sense.[11] As has been noted by James Doheny apropos of the release of *Kid A*, the band members «weren't nostalgic for past glories,» but

> you can be sure that their record company most certainly was. If they had been disappointed when they initially heard *OK Computer*, you can imagine what they thought on hearing *Kid A* for the first time. [...] Even worse, the band had decided that the album was to stand entirely on its own merits. There would be no singles, no videos, and relatively few interviews.[12]

Among the initiatives put forth by Radiohead in this regard, we limit ourselves here to mentioning just a few, like the unusual (at least in 2000) promotion method of *Kid A* through internet, evading the use of more traditional channels of communication like television and radio which were considered absolutely fundamental at the time to properly promote a new album,[13] or the free download of *In Rainbows* in 2017 through a «Pay what you want» program. Regarding this phenomenon – with a fleeting reference to Radiohead and also to other pop-rock musicians[14] – Alberto Mario Banti has observed that «[t]he spaces available to alternative forms of creativity are not utterly suffocated by the overbearing weight of big corporations and mainstream entertainment culture that they largely encourage,» and that the internet «offers potential opportunities to free oneself from the grasp of hegemonic narratives, if

---

11 On the complex question concerning the relation between Radiohead and the music industry, see the essays included in the third part of Forbes and Reisch 2009 (Milsky 2009; Tate 2009; Wittkower 2009).

12 Doheny 2002, p. 87.

13 «In a departure from industry practice,» on the occasion of the publication of *Kid A* (2000) «Radiohead released no singles and conducted few interviews and photoshoots. Instead, they released short animations and became one of the first major acts to use the internet for promotion. Bootlegs of early performances were shared on filesharing services, and *Kid A* was leaked before release. In 2000, Radiohead toured Europe in a custom-built tent without corporate logos» (https://en.wikipedia.org/wiki/Kid_A).

14 Banti 2017, p. 498.

one so wishes.[15]» Although it is certainly not possible to develop a complete sense of certainty about whether or not these opportunities are «truly a precondition for the birth of new discursive formations that have a social and ethical scope different from mainstream popular culture and that are also strong enough to challenge the hegemony of the mainstream,» it is anyway worth mentioning that, at least according to some scholars,

> the extremely rapid evolution of computer and media technologies is laying the groundwork for a new technological society that allows users of the internet, Facebook, Twitter, iPhones, iPads and the entire expanding galaxy of apps and software, to place themselves at the center of a convergent, interactive, participatory network that is open to grassroots changes that arrive from users or interpretive micro-communities.[16]

Applying these thoughts to Radiohead's catalog of music, we can say that especially *Kid A* is one of the most daring albums produced by the band and, as a whole, can be considered as a sort of musical «riot act» by a band that had been «a hitherto "front-line" rock act,[17]» as well as a musical experiment that, in its own way, was quite extreme and radical at the time, guided by the goal of freeing itself from the mindset of a homogenizing, standardized culture and the system of the music business.[18] The band's *No-Logo Tour* is quite emblematic and meaningful in this sense, as it was a series of concerts in which no advertising from brands or sponsors was featured, and in which Radiohead also jettisoned other marketing strategies.[19] Thom Yorke and his bandmates have always been quite honest about their discomfort with, and intolerance towards, a fixed, dominant, predetermined sociopolitical and cultural system. The cover art of *Kid A*, «which contains a hidden

---

15   Banti 2017, p. 501.
16   Banti 2017, p. 501.
17   Doheny 2002, p. 121. We freely use here the expression «riot act,» clearly borrowing it from the title of Pearl Jam's seventh album from 2002, precisely entitled *Riot Act*.
18   For a general comment about the songs of *Kid A*, see Doheny 2002, pp. 84-107; Franchi 2009, pp. 210-249.
19   On «Kid Activism,» that is, on the relation between *Kid A*'s aesthetics and political commitment, see Lin 2018, pp. 79-97.

booklet that can be taken out by removing the CD tray,[20]» depicts a complex enigma of allusive and metaphorical figures that are not so subtle representations of members of the British government, like the deformed, parodied caricature of former prime minister Tony Blair, for example.

In this sense, what seems to emerge from the band's dystopian scenario in *Kid A* is the image of an authoritarian world disguised as a democratic society in which the fatal combination of technology, alienation, reification, commodification and standardization contributes to the inception of the blinded, sluggish state human beings have sunk into, i.e. what we may call, following Horkheimer and Adorno, «a social context which induces blindness.[21]» In fact, what various critical philosophers of the 20th century have offered is fundamental a vision of contemporary individuals living in a condition of unfreedom or pseudo-freedom, convinced that there is a free choice between different possibilities that, however, in reality are not only standardized but also predetermined from the start. This implies, for such critical thinkers, that many people live in a sort of state of unawareness and blindness, controlled by, and subordinated to, the social system. For example, as Horkheimer and Adorno critically and pessimistically observe:

> The overripeness of society lives on the immaturity of the ruled. The more complex and sensitive the social, economic, and scientific mechanism, to the operation of which the system of production has long since attuned the body, the more impoverished are the experiences of which the body is capable. The elimination of qualities, their conversion into functions, is transferred by rationalized modes of work to the human capacity for experience, which tends to revert to that of amphibians. The regression of the masses today lies in their inability to hear with their own ears what has not already been heard, to touch with their hands what has not previously been grasped; it is the new form of blindness which supersedes that of vanquished myth. Through the mediation of the total society, which

---

20 Melissano 2003, p. 99.
21 Horkheimer and Adorno 2002, p. 33. For a general interpretation of Adorno's critique of the culture industry, in the context of what he (with Horkheimer) called the «administered world» and the «social context which induces blindness,» see Marino 2021b.

encompasses all relationships and impulses, human beings are being turned back into precisely what the developmental law of society, the principle of the self, had opposed: mere examples of the species, identical to one another through isolation within the compulsively controlled collectivity.[22]

Beside this, according to various philosophical conceptions of our techno-scientific contemporary world, it can be stated that, much like how «the modern individual seems (according to modern ideologies) isolated from his/her context, autonomous, independent without displaying connections to an invisible (social) whole, the functioning of which is totally hidden to the individual,» in a somehow comparable way «the technological object appears individual, simple, self sufficient,» whereas «around and behind [the technological object] there is actually a complex technological system, often multiple systems.[23]» This highlights how the human beings, if compared in this context to technological objects, are silently and unconsciously integrated into, and assimilated to, a much wider and obscure context, which is nonetheless determinant for all aspects of life as it is actually experienced in the present age. The sociopolitical system (for the human being) and the technological macro-network (for the technological object) offer multiple analogies in this sense: both control and monitor individuals as well as digital products, and according to such a view, the contemporary individual is just as subjugated and defined by the technological universe as by the sociopolitical system.

Is it possible to connect the music of a pop-rock band like Radiohead to the aforementioned intellectual discourses, defined up to this point by antagonistic characteristics that are in constant evolution? In a particular phase of their artistic career and history, at the turn of the millennium, the members of Radiohead decided to fully immerse themselves in the mindset of the existing and predominant system, which is to say the world of technology, to understand its processes and codes of expression in order to «spit out,» using technology's own language, our «digital anxieties,[24]»

---

22   Horkheimer and Adorno 2002, pp. 28-29.
23   Nacci 2000, pp. 142-143.
24   Alfieri 2019, p. 69.

in the same way that the contemporary individuals find themselves surrounded by, and subordinate to, a socio-political and economic system whose ideology glorifies and imposes the potentialities presented by technology. So, returning to the questions we discussed earlier, just like the «technocentric» social system – according to the pessimistic and sometimes veritably dystopian vision that seems to emerge from certain songs of the first phase of Radiohead's aesthetics discussed in the previous chapter – silently controls and directs the individuals, conditioning them in their fundamental decisions, the relation with technology has also shaped Radiohead's musical development. In light of what we could emphatically and ambitiously call Radiohead's musical *Kehre* (clearly borrowing this concept from the terminology usually employed to define a specific and unique phase of Heidegger's path of thinking[25]), fueled by a nonconformist desire to stray from a predetermined path, the band's musical production is now wrapped, enveloped, and conditioned by the rigid and rigorous processes of technology. The latter glitters in all of its authority and reveals its twofold identity from the outset, which lies in its being a potential instrument of subjugation as well as a potential means of human emancipation.

Operating on a musical level that is also rich with philosophical suggestions, after *OK Computer* Radiohead consciously funneled certain features that are typical of technology into the band's work, bringing to light the different (and sometimes opposing, indeed) results that technology can achieve in various contexts. From this

---

25 The concept of *Kehre* refers to the «turn» in Heidegger's thought that occurred in the mid 1930s, according to an interpretation that has by now become rather canonical in the field of Heidegger studies – although it is not our intention to support a rigidly dualist concept of Heidegger's *Denkweg* that «divides [it] into two antipodes, an existential-anthropological one and an ontological one,» nor to replicate «the *topos* of a Heidegger I and II» that are radically different, «one focused on existence, the other on Being» (Mazzarella 1987, pp. 21, 90). To put it simply, and certainly recognizing that such a comparison with Heidegger is obviously quite bold, it seems possible to make an emphatic reference to the notion of *Kehre* to underline how, for Radiohead, starting with the band's third album, *OK Computer*, there was an evident «turn,» which is to say a shift, a leap, a stylistic evolution towards musical experimentation, in terms of form, style and content.

point of view, what we have defined so far as a the second phase of Radiohead's musical path is the stage in which technology deeply penetrated the music of the band in a manner that is in some ways unprecedented (especially in light of the overall context of the music scene of the 1990s), challenging the expressive and stylistic paradigms attributable to Radiohead up until that point and, more generally, encouraging a veritable transformation of the identity of pop-rock music as such. As Radiohead's fans certainly know, this specifically happened through the unexpected addition of an original technological and electronic component in the music of a band that, as we said in the previous chapter, up until that point had presented itself as a relatively traditional and therefore «reassuring» classic pop-rock group, especially in the albums *Pablo Honey* and *The Bends*, whereas *OK Computer* had already started to introduce some original deviations and intriguing experimentations that can be viewed retrospectively as apparently foreshadowing the band's transition to a new musical phase.[26]

The new and complex electronic sounds of Radiohead, first in *Kid A* and shortly after in *Amnesiac*, represent the only means of expression permitted at that stage: one that can sometimes evoke oppressive, overwhelming, almost suffocating sensations, but that also appears to disclose the only path that could enable the band to impressively and emblematically express its unique message at that point in its career. In short, it is as if, in this second stage of Radiohead's musical development, technology itself speaks through the five members of the band, who thus appear as «ventriloquists» (to use Radiohead's own words from the song «Kid A») endowed with a powerful sound, a convincing voice and an ability to find new ways to express their own subjectivity *without* merely placing themselves in contrast to the cold and calculating objectivity of technology, but rather immersing themselves in technology and allowing it to deeply permeate the band's creative method.

---

26   As has been noted, «[a]ll music may be hybrid, but *OK Computer* seemed a clear turning point for Radiohead's brand of hybridization: this time, it was as much about the sounds as the approach. [...] [E]verything changed once *OK Computer* proved both critically and financially successful» (Lin 2018, pp. 61, 81).

Should we want to deduce some philosophical consequences and implications of these procedures and choices – that, in principle, are not connected to philosophy in the strict sense, but only to the different musical options and strategies adopted by a pop-rock band –, we could speak of a transition or even a turning point, in a certain sense. In fact, what this phase of Radiohead's career shows is a shift from a predominantly negative perception of technology – *only* seen as a subjugating, alienating, dominating and suffocating entity against the expressive needs of what we can call the «soul» – to a more complex, nuanced and sophisticated view of technology. From this new perspective, technology now appears to Radiohead as a dimension that, while certainly equipped with some aspects and shades that may appear obscure, threatening and alienating, is *no longer* associated in a dualist and Manichaeist way only with «evil» (in comparison to the sphere of human expressivity or «soul,» supposedly understood as unconditionally «good» or, in any case, as a safe and guaranteed reservoir of sincerity, spontaneity and authenticity). So, the aim is now to understand technology in its complexity and twofoldness, attempting to use it to autonomously fulfill one's own needs rather than only feeling subjugated by technology as a merely heteronomous force.

According to Alessandro Alfieri, the use of an experimental and technological musical language represents a concrete manifestation of «the intuition that would determine Radiohead's career.[27]» In fact, it was thanks to this intuition that, after a period of creative crisis and stasis after the completion of its second album, the band was able to «reintroduce itself in an uncompromisingly specific way» in the music scene between the end of the 1990s and the beginning of the new millennium: «for Radiohead, experimentation became an opportunity to avoid succumbing to self-destructive nihilism[28]» (with which Alfieri refers to a distinctive feature of a large part of contemporary pop-rock music, especially in the so-called grunge scene), so as to *not* let the creative energy of the band crumble and dissolve, as had happened for many bands of the same period that quickly disappeared from the spotlight. In other words, it was thanks to this ability to change its relationship

---

27   Alfieri 2019, p. 65.
28   Alfieri 2019, p. 66.

with technology and, in doing so, musically «shed its skin,» that
Radiohead was able to «create an aesthetics and an imaginary
freed from the trap of becoming retro» (which was the case, vice-
versa, for many Britpop bands of that time), on the one hand, and
freed from a mere «dramatic existentialism,» on the other hand,
thus becoming «a source of inspiration for many rock bands that
would follow.[29]» As we will discuss in the last chapter, due to their
unique aesthetics Radiohead also became a point of reference for
many jazz and even avant-garde musicians, carving out a truly
unique space in today's music scene.

Starting with *Kid A* (although, as we said, there was likely some
meaningful foreshadowing on *OK Computer*), Radiohead found
a new voice and a new horizon, when the band decided to devote
itself to what had been previously considered simply the «muddy
water» of technology. Despite the fact that it still often appears as
a threat and a potential source of alienation, technology nonetheless seems to now offer new opportunities and original potentialities for the band to make use of, making it aesthetically legitimate
to follow its logic and rules. It is through this explicit and direct
relation with the world of technology, and not through a strategy
of «escape» or «evasion» (i.e., avoiding all contact with technology), that the malaise, frustration and nihilism of the contemporary age are able to emerge and be brutally reflected and expressed
in Radiohead's songs, with the awareness that a «human» message
can often be more powerful and effective precisely when it is con-
veyed through technological means and their (real or presumed)
«dehumanizing» nature.

This was an inner revolution for Radiohead that was naturally
not free from consequences. Indeed, the band restructured and
almost entirely revolutionized its compositional process, adopting new musical references – usually artists belonging to the electronic music scene, both new and old, like in the case of Brian Eno
and Paul Lansky – and grappling with new methodologies and approaches to artistic creation. The sound of the band, as proposed
by Radiohead's lead singer, was remodeled with an electronic
base and sampled sounds that are modified in the studio through
computers: Yorke «began to bring the band rhythms, sounds and

---

29   Alfieri 2019, p. 68.

textures around which their new music could coalesce.[30]» Even the band's approach in the recording studio itself radically changed: Radiohead heavily experimented now with the effects of original, relatively unknown and usually digital instruments. «Everything was open for reassessment during this process, with absolutely nothing sacred. At one stage, the band was split into two separate composing/production units who were both forbidden to touch guitars or drums.[31]» The title of an article in an issue of *Rolling Stone* from that time is particularly illustrative: «In order to save themselves, Radiohead had to destroy rock 'n' roll.[32]»

3.

It is possible to briefly introduce here a new comparison between Radiohead and Adorno. In fact, in 1949, with the publication of his musicological masterpiece *Philosophy of Modern Music* (a book articulated in two essays, dedicated respectively to Arnold Schönberg and Igor Stravinsky), Adorno wrote, in reference to Schönberg, that «[t]welve-tone technique is truly the fate of music. It enchains music in liberating it.[33]» In an attempt to establish a daring but, in our view, not implausible parallel between Adorno's position on the twelve-tone technique and the new technologized style used by Radiohead on *Kid A*, we could describe also Radiohead's music as «radical» (at least in reference to the mainstream pop-rock music scene), its «technical structural law of music» coherently corresponding to «[t]he seismographic registration of traumatic shock,» and its «[m]usical language» being «polarized according to its extremes: towards gestures of shock resembling bodily convulsions on the one hand, and on the other towards a crystalline standstill of a human being whom anxiety causes to freeze in her tracks.[34]»

To be clear: we in no way wish to draw audacious and ambitious parallels, believing them to be unconditionally founded and

---

30   Doheny 2002, p. 86.
31   Doheny 2002, p. 86.
32   Doheny 2002, pp. 86-87.
33   Adorno 2016, p. 45.
34   Adorno 2016, p. 27.

absolute, between the music of Radiohead and Schönberg (based on Adorno's interpretation). However, with such a comparison we nonetheless aim to show how, in both cases, following the path of technological composition led to a revolution in the traditional ways of thinking about music. As different and incomparable as the use of the musical material in the two areas of «serious music» (Schönberg) and «popular music» (Radiohead) may be, it can be said anyway that in both cases, at a certain point, a choice was made to elaborate and structure the musical material in a manner based on exact norms and rules, which is to say the conception of «rational total organization of the total musical material,[35]» in which «[a]ccuracy or correctness, as a mathematical hypothesis, takes the place of that element called "the idea" in traditional art.[36]» In saying this, it is important to consider that, in the case of the electronic sound developed by Radiohead after *Kid A*, a digital sound represents an elaboration and (approximate) measurement of an analog sound signal through a computer or sampler, something that clearly cannot be applied to Schönberg's twelve-tone technique as it surely widens the possibilities of the musical artwork beyond the limits imposed by the tonal system, but nonetheless remaining within the limits of a compositional technique that offers a limited choice of sounds among the twelve available tones of the equal temperament chromatic scale.

About Schönberg's twelve-tone technique, Adorno famously writes: «A system by which music dominates nature results. It reflects a longing present since the beginning of the bourgeois era: to "grasp" and to place all sounds into an order, and to reduce the magic essence of music to human logic.[37]» The philosophical, musicological and also sociological implications of Adorno's view – starting with the notion of «domination of nature» itself, which constitutes one of the fundamental pillars of Adorno's thinking in all its various branches and facets[38] – are vast and various, and clearly go beyond the limited scope of a book on the «philosophy of Radiohead.» However, the aforementioned

---

35   Adorno 2016, p. 35.
36   Adorno 2016, p. 44.
37   Adorno 2016, p. 43.
38   On the role played by the question of nature in Adorno's dialectical thinking, see Cook 2011.

passage from Adorno's *Philosophy of Modern Music*, if properly understood and adapted to the context of the present investigation, can also help us understand how Radiohead's technological turn in *Kid A* apparently takes on the connotations of a sort of conscious indulgence (and therefore actively desired, rather than passively experienced) of technology's control on human action. As such, this turn, precisely through this indulgence and appropriation of technology to offer new opportunities to the individual's expressive needs, upon closer analysis seems to dialectically reverse itself into a new (additional, more conscious) desire for human control over technology by fully adopting it as one of its instruments.

To push the analogy between the atonal/dodecaphonic music of Schönberg and the music of Radiohead (specifically in the second phase of the band's artistic evolution) much further would be inappropriate and haphazard, as they are musical phenomena characterized by overwhelming differences in terms of personality, context, background, style, cultural references and much more. What this digression aims to do is rather to offer a brief reflection on how both figures, when faced with forms of malaise and alienation that apparently characterized their respective historical periods, chose *not* to take a reassuring (but, upon closer examination, deceptive) «step back» towards the reestablishment of musical codes and styles apparently cloaked in naturalness and authenticity (but, in actuality, ineffective, impotent, historically discredited, and fatally decayed into clichés), but instead opted to suspend and finally overcome certain traditional conceptions and forms of expression, in order to take a «step forward» rather than a «step back.» Notwithstanding all the obvious differences between figures like Schönberg and Radiohead, in both cases it is nevertheless possible to observe a similar decision to seriously, lucidly and consciously adopt new techniques in a systematic manner, considering the traditional forms and musical means of expression insufficient, or no longer able, to express that which unyieldingly requires to be expressed.

In his philosophical interpretation of the adventures of 20th-century *neue Musik*, Adorno famously claims: «All forms of music, not just those of Expressionism, are realizations of content. [...] The forms of art reflect the history of man more truthfully than do documents themselves. Every ossification of form insists that it be interpreted as the negation of the severity of life.[39]» Relating all of this – in a certainly interpretive manner – to the specific case of the aesthetics of Radiohead and, in particular, to the «ossification of form» that we find in tracks of *Kid A* and *Amnesiac* such as «Idioteque» or «I Might Be Wrong,» we can suggest that such an attempt at rationalization based on new musical technologies aimed to communicate certain inner expressive processes of the human «soul» with greater effectiveness and pathos compared to the band's seemingly more «natural» and «authentic» albums like *Pablo Honey* or *The Bends* (which, precisely due to this, when listened to today, probably and paradoxically sound more «inauthentic» than *Kid A* and *Amnesiac*).

4.

As we said, the style of *Kid A*, the band's fourth album and the veritable groundbreaking moment in its career, inaugurated a new phase in Radiohead's aesthetics. From this point of view, *Kid A* is a work that can be truly defined as unique in the context of Radiohead's musical development (and not only). As has been noted:

> *Kid A* was political yet visceral, thoughtful yet abstracted, assured yet contradictory; it served as both a musical breakthrough for its fans and a hybridized pastiche for its critics; it was actively critiqued, not passively consumed; it was an assimilated cultural aberration that wouldn't stop grumbling, a subversion of capitalism that ultimately produced a lot of capital [...]. *Kid A* could be seen as Radiohead's opportunity to construct a new identity, to pacify a desire for change because stasis would've meant tailspinning into the same predictable cycles [...]. Despite the uncertainty in direction, Radiohead realized that aesthetic renewal would necessitate a renewed approach. [...] The album has the distinction of being Radiohead's most emotionally, intellectually, and musically challenging work. [...] But unlike many current «experimental» artists, who dutifully avoid harmony and rhythm to be labeled as such, Radiohead ex-

---

39   Adorno 2016, p. 27.

perimented with both new sounds *and* approaches while remaining quintessentially «Radiohead.[40]»

Kid A can at times sound difficult, hard, hostile, angular, indirect and intentionally tending towards a strong negation of every attempt at conciliation between the individual and his/her world – a sense of conciliation that typically seems to be more characteristic of commercial pop songs, which adhere more strongly to the usual expectations and listening habits of the masses, and which tend to reiterate and confirm certain clichés rather than surprise the listeners and disorient them with dissonances and irreconcilable sonorities. The sounds used on *Kid A* are dark and threatening, and the themes discussed in various songs allude to a contemporary dystopia inhabited by a sort of new «generation A» of the 21st century. The title track, number two on the songlist of *Kid A*, is at first listen completely different from what the band had produced up to that point. The song «Kid A» is a sort of «musical fantasy[41]» entirely composed of sounds produced by bizarre and unusual electronic instruments which contribute to defining the song's absurd and unsettling atmosphere. These sounds almost make the lyrics incomprehensible and indecipherable, and one may suspect that the latter were used «mainly for their sonic properties,[42]» although it is interesting to examine the rather unique meaning of certain lines like: «Rats and children follow me out of town. Come on kids.[43]» The electronic sounds that create a soundscape as extravagant as it is unsettling are from toy instruments that may remind of «the sonic scene of [a] musical *Toy Story*,[44]» although the most surreal instrument in this track is definitively the lead singer's voice, entirely filtered by a Vocoder that renders the lyrics dark, enigmatic and indecipherable: «We've got heads on sticks and you've got ventriloquists.[45]» From this point of view, one can observe that on *Kid A*, beside adopting «new lyrical technique[s],» like «cut-up lyrics,» which made «*Kid A*'s lyrics [...] often read like

---

40   Lin 2018, pp. 1, 25, 31, 73.
41   Doheny 2002, p. 91.
42   Doheny 2002, p. 92.
43   Radiohead 2017, p. 131.
44   Doheny 2002, p. 92.
45   Radiohead 2017, p. 130.

Dada poetry,» «like detached allusions [and] impressionistic encryptions,» Thom Yorke even arrived to seek

> to alter the very color of his voice, what one might call Radiohead's bread and butter, their *je ne sais quoi*, their It factor. With new sequencers, new recording software (Pro Tools, Cubase, Auto-Tune, Logic), and a new frame of mind, Thom was able to dislocate his voice *ad infinitum*, to obscure its emotive signifiers and emphasize texture, to reposition it from a privileged status to just another instrument.[46]

Regarding these lyrics and the vocal processing used in the album, a statement by Thom Yorke is particularly interesting: «On "Kid A," the lyrics are absolutely brutal and horrible and I wouldn't be able to sing them straight. But talking them and having them vocodered... so that I wasn't even responsible for the melody... that was great, it felt like you're not answerable to this thing.[47]» It is certainly just as illustrative to mention some remarks from Jonny Greenwood, one of the band's two guitarists: «a voice into a microphone onto a tape, onto a CD and through your speakers is all as illusory and as fake as any synthesiser – it doesn't put Thom in your front room. But one is perceived as "real," the other somehow "unreal." It's the same with guitars versus samplers. It was just freeing to discard the notion of acoustic sounds being truer.[48]»

The provocative message that is «hostile» to the «hostility» of technology (according to our interpretive approach, deeply inspired by the conceptions of technology offered by various protagonists of 20th-century philosophy) is thus expressed in *Kid A* with greater freedom, effectiveness and «human» expressivity, precisely by making use of, and being filtered through, the «dehumanizing» nature of digital technologies. With those statements, Yorke and Greenwood emphasize the advantages and potentialities that certain electronic devices can offer in an attempt to communicate

---

46   Lin 2018, pp. 17, 19-21.
47   Yorke, cited in Doheny 2002, p. 92. On the lyrics of *Kid A* – also in comparison to *The Bends* and *OK Computer* – and Yorke's particular processes of lyric composition and performance on this record, see Lin 2018, pp. 14-22.
48   Greenwood, cited in Doheny 2002, pp. 92-93. On the same topic, see also Lin 2018, pp. 36-37.

the band's «unfiltered» thoughts, as the electronic device, in this sense, is already a «filter» for truth. Following this logic, technology can be viewed as the veil under which true reality lies. It is this veil that causes reality to acquire a characteristic, altered and technologized aspect, and reality, in order to be brought to light and fully understood, requires that the omnipresent mediation of technology in the human relation to the world *not* be cast aside or placed in brackets, but that the two openly interact, that the human mind assimilates and intentionally transforms technology into an instrument in order to express and speak aloud what would otherwise remain forever in the sphere of the unexpressed and unspoken (if not the inexpressible and unspeakable as such).

5.

In light of Greenwood's aforementioned statement on the illusion of a supposedly «natural» character of music played with acoustic instruments (if compared to electronic and technological sounds), it is possible to establish a new connection with Adorno's thinking. This is *not* solely based on the fact that Adorno critically considered popular music, as we said, as a mere commodity, a vehicle of illusions, and a damaging «social cement[49]» for a society that should be demystified and dismantled to its roots rather than strengthened and «cementified.» Beside this, we are also referring here to the fact that Adorno centered a part of his critique of popular music on the latter's «natural» (or better, pseudo-natural) character, understood as a necessary requirement to «plug» it and thus ensure its popularity. For Adorno, indeed,

> Popular music must simultaneously meet two demands. One is for stimuli that provoke the listener's attention. The other is for the material to fall within the category of what the musically untrained listener would call «natural» music: that is, the sum total of all the conventions and material formulas in music to which he is accustomed and which he regards as the inherent, simple language of music itself, no matter how late the development might be which pro-

---

49   Adorno 2009, pp. 315-319.

duced this natural language. [...] Extravagances are tolerated only insofar as they can be recast into the so-called natural language. In terms of consumer-demand, the standardization of popular music is only the expression of this dual desideratum imposed upon it by the musical frame of mind of the public – that it be «stimulatory» by deviating in some way from the established «natural,» and that it maintain the supremacy of the natural against such deviations. The attitude of the audience toward the natural language is reinforced by standardized production, which institutionalizes desiderata which originally might have come from the public.[50]

Today, much like in the years in which Adorno wrote his main works on the culture industry, the dominant mindset and the «affirmative» culture (as intended by Marcuse[51]) seem to wish to propagate the conviction that in general everything is «alright,» «under control» and «in its right place.» One may be tempted to object to this conviction with Adorno's words, that in truth «[t]he whole is the false[52]» and, with Radiohead's words, that a sentence like «everything [is] in its right place» does *not* sound in any way honest or plausible, due to the fact that in the present

---

50   Adorno 2009, p. 287.
51   This is primarily a reference to the well known essay by Marcuse from 1937, «The Affirmative Character of Culture» (see Marcuse 2006).
52   Adorno 2005, § 29, p. 50. More precisely, Adorno's famous statement should be translated as «the whole (*das Ganze*) is the untrue (*das Unwahre*),» in order to properly express the dialectical opposition between truth and untruth. As Adorno explains elsewhere, in order to clarify his (Hegelian and at the same time anti-Hegelian) thesis: «the rationality of [the] consolidation into a totality is itself irrationality, the totality of the negative. "The whole is the untrue," not merely because the thesis of totality is itself untruth, being the principle of domination inflated to the absolute; the idea of a positivity that can master everything that opposes it through the superior power of a comprehending spirit is the mirror image of the experience of the superior coercive force inherent in everything that exists by virtue of its consolidation under domination. This is the truth in Hegel's untruth. The force of the whole, which it mobilizes, is not a mere fantasy on the part of spirit; it is the force of the real web of illusion in which all individual existence remains trapped. By specifying, in opposition to Hegel, the negativity of the whole, philosophy satisfies, for the last time, the postulate of determinate negation, which is a positing. The ray of light that reveals the whole to be untrue in all its moments is none other than utopia, the utopia of the whole truth, which is still to be realized» (Adorno 1993, pp. 87-88).

age little to nothing actually seems to be «in its right place.» From this point of view, insisting on this association between Adorno and Radiohead, and following certain suggestions on the relation between artworks and commodities from Frankfurt critical theorists, one is tempted to suggest that, much like a musical composition that aims to take a stand against certain flaws of a hyper-technological world *cannot* exempt itself from a direct confrontation with technological experimentation (and, indeed, must make use of this experimentation to reach its purposes), also a work of art that aims to criticize the growing commodification of culture and existence *cannot* exclude a lucid and self-conscious confrontation with these commodification processes. Rather, it must deal with this risk, incorporating it into its own structure and transcending it in the immanence of the artwork's form.

In *Aesthetic Theory* Adorno emphatically defined the work of art as a thing (a *res*, in Latin) that is able to transcend its reity or «thingness,» nonetheless remaining on a dimension of immanence, and thus able to reveal the «nonexistent,» evidently still limited by the totality of the existing world. Indeed, for Adorno «[a]rtworks are things that tend to slough off their reity. [...] The spirit of artworks is constituted in their reity, and their reity, the existence of works, originates in their spirit.[53]» As Adorno clarifies in various passages of his *Aesthetic Theory*:

> what is unreal and nonexistent in art is not independent of reality. It is not arbitrarily posited, not invented, as is commonly thought; rather, it is structured by proportions between what exists, propor-

---

53   Adorno 2002a, p. 277. Within the same context, compare also these passages: «Every artwork is in fact an oxymoron. Its own reality is for it unreal, it is indifferent to what it essentially is, and at the same time it is its own precondition; in the context of reality it is all the more unreal and chimerical. [...] An artwork is real only to the extent that, as an artwork, it is unreal, self-sufficient, and differentiated from the empirical world, of which it nevertheless remains a part. But its unreality – its determination as spirit – only exists to the extent that it has become real; nothing in an artwork counts that is not there in an individuated form. In aesthetic semblance the artwork takes up a stance toward reality, which it negates by becoming a reality *sui generis*. Art protests against reality by its own objectivation» (Adorno 2002a, p. 279).

tions that are themselves defined by what exists, its deficiency, distress, and contradictoriness as well as its potentialities; even in these proportions real contexts resonate. Art is related to its other as is a magnet to a field of iron filings. [...] The appearance of the nonexistent as if it existed motivates the question as to the truth of art. By its form alone art promises what is not; it registers objectively, however refractedly, the claim that because the nonexistent appears it must indeed be possible. [...] Although the nonexisting emerges suddenly in artworks, they do not lay hold of it bodily as with the pass of a magic wand. The nonexisting is mediated to them through fragments of the existing, which they assemble into an apparition. It is not for art to decide by its existence if the nonexisting that appears indeed exists as something appearing or remains semblance. As figures of the existing, unable to summon into existence the nonexisting, artworks draw their authority from the reflection they compel on how they could be the overwhelming image of the nonexisting if it did not exist in itself.[54]

According to Adorno, an artwork is always a *res* but provided with an addendum («the more[55]») that allows it to transcend its basic reified character and to become a sort of self-transcending *res* – a thing that is «more» than just a thing, as it were.[56] This is in some ways analogous (and, clearly, it frees us in part from Adorno's totalizing refusal of *all* mass culture, including *all* popular music[57]) to what we believe in the field of pop-rock music can be considered the potentiality of certain commodities to momentarily suspend and transcend their own commodity status: commodities that transcend themselves or, to speak, self-transcending commodities. In fact, works of the popular arts are surely conditioned by the context that they belong to – and hence by the culture industry as an organ of what Adorno called «the administered world» – but are nevertheless *not fully*

---

54   Adorno 2002a, pp. 7, 82, 83.
55   Adorno 2002a, pp. 78-84.
56   Adorno 2002a, pp. 174-175.
57   As has been noted, indeed, from an orthodox Adornian perspective «the musics developed by the culture industries are *all* commodified musics and their appeal to the subject works *in the same way* as that of *all* commodities» (Witkin 2000, p. 155): «in radio, the film industry, the variety act, cartoons – *everywhere* – Adorno saw the culture industry as the enemy of humanity and true feeling» (Witkin 1998, p. 173).

determined by it, and are therefore capable, at least in principle, to partially transcend it.[58]

In a sense, aesthetically successful pop-rock songs can be understood as works that, performing a sort of aesthetic acrobatic turn, succeed in doing what Adorno himself self-consciously and paradoxically prescribed to philosophy and art in the age of their potential «liquidation,» namely to be able to repeat the Baron Münchhausen's gesture of «pulling himself out of the bog by his pig-tail»: «nothing less is asked of the thinker today than that he [or she] should be at every moment both within things and outside them.[59]» In an attempt to find an *ad hoc* conceptualization, we could say that, in a similar way, nothing less is asked of the pop-rock musician today than that he/she should be able to work «in the marketplace but not governed by the values of the marketplace[60]» (citing again Robert Fripp's penetrating maxim), struggling to compose and perform non-standardized music that nevertheless must start from the culture industry's standardized norms and thus must transcend them – more or less like the «cognitive utopia» of negative dialectics, for Adorno, requires «to use concepts to unseal the non-conceptual with concepts, without making it their equal.[61]» In our view, Radiohead's most successful works have been able to fully respect the value and meaning of Fripp's aforementioned «golden rule.»

6.

Returning now to Radiohead, we can say that the illusory nature of the social system and the norms that govern it was strongly perceived and expressed by the band in the second phase of its career, becoming a spokesperson for this dissent in an attempt to demystify the actual social situation. In this sense, it is no coincidence that

---

58	According to Adorno, «[i]n the midst of a world dominated by utility, art indeed has a utopic aspect as the other of this world, as exempt from the mechanism of the social process of production and reproduction» (Adorno 2002a, p. 311).
59	Adorno 2005, § 46, p. 74.
60	Fripp, cited in Tamm 1990, p. 92.
61	Adorno 2004, p. 10.

Kid A opens with the track «Everything in Its Right Place,» with an almost jarring, paradoxical title when compared to the non-conformist and critical content of the band's songs. Indeed, this minimalist song is «so affecting, so wonderfully impassioned,[62]» an attempt to «finally get back home to [the] "right place"» (as musically testified by «[t]he journey the chords make in this piece»), «whatever that might be,[63]» but with the lingering sensation that *not* everything is going well, i.e. things are actually *not* in their «right place.» A few chords from an electric piano open the piece, the same chords that form the skeleton of nearly the entire song, above which first the verses sung by Thom Yorke unfurl, hypnotically playing the same sampled sentence on repeat («Everything, everything, in its right place[64]»), as if it were a mantra. This esoteric and hypnotic atmosphere is accentuated by the digital and sampled sounds in the background.

The song has few, repetitive lyrics, and after the first verse Yorke repeats the enigmatic phrase: «Yesterday I woke up sucking a lemon.[65]» This image recalls the phase of a physical (and spiritual) awakening that consists of an abrupt, almost disgusted, reaction when faced with the renewed contact with reality one experiences upon waking, perhaps the result of gaining awareness or a permanent feeling of malaise. In an attempt to boldly suggest a free and imaginative comparison between pop-rock music and literature, we are tempted to critically compare and contrast the bitter, lemon-flavored awakening described by Yorke in «Everything in Its Right Place,» and the sweet awakening dripping with «involuntary memory» narrated by Marcel Proust in the well known story of the *madeleine* from Combray, in the first part of *Swann's Way*, the first volume of *Remembrance of Things Past*. Here, indeed, Proust famously writes:

> the pictures which [voluntary memory, the memory of the intellect] shows us preserve nothing of the past itself [...]. There is a large element of chance in these matters, and a second chance occurrence, that of our own death, often prevents us from awaiting for any

---

62 Doheny 2002, p. 91.
63 Doheny 2002, p. 90.
64 Radiohead 2017, p. 128.
65 Radiohead 2017, p. 128.

length of time that favours of the first. [...] And so it is with our own past. It is a labour in vain to attempt to recapture it: all the efforts of our intellect must prove futile. The past is hidden somewhere outside the realm, beyond the reach of intellect, in some material object (in which the sensation which that material object will give us) of which we have no inkling. And it depends on chance whether or not we come upon this object before we ourselves must die.[66]

Then, in the same chapter of *Swann's Way*, Proust goes on to narrate and observes:

Many years had elapsed during which nothing of Combray, save what was comprised in the theatre and the drama of my going to bed there, had any existence for me, when one day in winter, on my return home, my mother, seeing that I was cold, offered me some tea, a thing I did not ordinarily take. I declined at first, and then, for no particular reason, changed my mind. She sent for one of those squat, plump little cakes called «petites madeleines,» which look as though they had been moulded in the fluted valve of a scallop shell. And soon, mechanically, dispirited after a dreary day with the prospect of a depressing morrow, I raised to my lips a spoonful of the tea in which I had soaked a morsel of the cake. No sooner had the warm liquid mixed with the crumbs touched my palate than a shiver ran through me and I stopped, intent upon the extraordinary thing that was happening to me. An exquisite pleasure had invaded my senses, something isolated, detached, with no suggestion of its origin. And at once the vicissitudes of life had become indifferent to me, its disasters innocuous, its brevity illusory – this new sensation having had on me the effect which love has of filling me with a precious essence; or rather this essence was not in me, it *was* me. I had ceased now to feel mediocre, contingent, mortal. Whence could it have come to me, this all-powerful joy? [...] Whence did it come? What did it mean? How could I seize and apprehend it? [...] It is plain that the truth I am seeking lies not in the cup but in myself. The drink has called it into being, but does not know it, and can only repeat indefinitely, with a progressive diminution of strength, the same message which I cannot interpret [...]. I being again to ask myself what it could have been, this unremembered state which brought with it no logical proof, but

---

66   Proust 1981, pp. 47-48.

the indisputable evidence, of its felicity, its reality, and in whose presence other states of consciousness melted and vanished. [...] And suddenly the memory revealed itself. The taste was that of the little piece of madeleine which on Sunday mornings at Combray (because on those mornings I did not go out before mass), when I went to say good morning to her in her bedroom, my aunt Léonie used to give me, dipping it first in her own cup of tea or tisane. [...] [W]hen from a long-distant past nothing subsists, after the people are dead, after the things are broken and scattered, taste and smell alone, more fragile but more enduring, more unsubstantial, more persistent, more faithful, remain poised a long time, like souls, re-membering, waiting, hoping, amid the ruins of all the rest; and bear unflinchingly, in the tiny and almost impalpable drop of their essence, the vast structure of recollection.[67]

Returning to the relation between art, technology and society, according to some philosophical positions that emerged in the 20th century «technology's presence is silent, invisible,[68]» and it numbs the individual in daily life through routine and predeter-mined behaviors. In this case, the main thesis is that technology is equipped with its own internal logic that acts against the hu-man being, possessing an intrinsic rationality that quickly tends to manifest itself as a form of irrationality,[69] what Jacques Ellul calls *déraison:* «the most rational system that has ever existed ac-centuates maladjustments and social obstructions, a system that marginalizes.[70]» From these philosophical perspectives (undoubt-edly authoritative and able to offer original points of reflection and fruitful insights, even if they risk sometimes to lead to exces-sive positions of «technophobia»), today we live in an irrational technocracy that, disguising its true nature through the reiterated proclamation of values like freedom and equality (passing them off as real and realized, rather than revealing them to be simply illusory), pushes for consensus and passive acceptance at all costs, as well as the elimination of criticism and dissent, causing indi-viduals to maintain a false and inauthentic attitude of optimism,

---

67   Proust 1981, pp. 48-50.
68   Nacci 2000, pp. 137-138.
69   Nacci 2000, p. 170.
70   Nacci 2000, pp. 173-174 (with specific reference to Ellul).

which is in line with what Radiohead seems to suggest in many of its songs, especially in *Kid A*.

Indeed, the sixth track of *Kid A* is entitled «Optimistic,» characterized by dense riffs and a guitar that makes use of a more traditional sound. The title, like «Everything in Its Right Place,» seems to make use of a sarcastic tone that quickly fades into pessimism. However, it can also be seen as expressing a certain comfort, an individual encouragement that is reinforced by the lyrics of the chorus: «If you try the best you can, if you try the best you can, / The best you can is good enough.[71]» These lines can be interpreted as allusions to a honest and personal attempt to act with the best intentions and with an awareness of the limited abilities of each individual, owing to the unavoidable restrictions and finitude of human nature. Yet, these same words can also seem empty and canned, mere slogans sold as corporate motivations only interested in promoting the blind pseudo-optimistic march of progress that also conceals the seed of regression (as in the famous interpretation offered by Horkheimer and Adorno, for whom today «progress is reverting to regression» and «cunning [...] reverts to stupidity[72]») and the seemingly painless adaptation of the individual to society (that actually comes at a great cost). The song is

---

71   Radiohead 2017, p. 135.

72   Horkheimer and Adorno 2002, pp. XVIII, 53. In the terminology used in *Dialectic of Enlightenment*, the fundamental tasks of critical theory can be summarized in the well known expression «[m]yth is already enlightenment and enlightenment reverts to mythology,» and in the idea that, «[i]f enlightenment does not assimilate reflection on [its] regressive moment, it seals its own fate» (Horkheimer and Adorno 2002, pp. XVI, XVIII). Indeed, according to Frankfurt critical theorists, the only form of unity that holds together the different moments of human history and civilization, that are otherwise fragmented and disjointed, is domination, which extends and transforms the «mastery over things» into a mastery over «the life and consciousness of human beings» (Horkheimer and Adorno 2002, p. 33). This is to say that, for critical theorists, ultimately reason proves to be today a sort of «rationalized irrationality» (Horkheimer 2004, p. 65): that is, a powerful means of adaptation for human self-preservation that, however, contrary to all expectations, ends up dialectically reversed as its opposite, an instrument of human self-destruction and maladjustment. As Horkheimer critically observes in *Eclipse of Reason*, although humanity has apparently entered an age of almost complete rationalization and technification, «[i]rrationality still molds the fate of men» (Horkheimer 2004, p. 106).

filled with allusions and references to Orwell's beast fable *Animal Farm*, like in the lyrics «fodder for the animals, / Living on animal farm,[73]» and outlines a prehistoric context ruled by the law that the bigger eat the smaller («The big fish eat the little ones, the big fish eat the little ones, / Not my problem, give me some[74]»), in a manner that is not unlike what continues to happen in late capitalist, hyper-technological societies that are however unable to free themselves from such ancestral and «inhuman» paradigms, and therefore unable to become truly «human» societies. In terms of both the form (i.e., the music) and the contents (i.e., the lyrics), this song is unsettling and evocative, with dark images and provocative negative metaphors, leading us to once again reflect on Adorno's idea that, in a world like ours, true art *cannot* be peaceful, affirmative and submissive:

> The decline of art in a false order is itself false. Its truth is the denial of the submissiveness into which its central principle – that of consistent correctness – has driven it. As long as art, which is constituted according to the categories of mass production, contributes to this ideology, and as long as artistic technique is a technique of repression, that other, functionless art has its own function. [...] By presenting the unreconciled picture of reality, it becomes incommensurable with this reality. In this way it expresses opposition to the injustice of the just verdict.[75]

The songs on *Kid A* can seem rather complex and counterintuitive, at least for listeners of pop-rock music that only search for what Benjamin called «[r]eception in distraction» that is characteristic of the contemporary age and that, according to Benjamin, «is increasingly noticeable in all areas of art and is a symptom of profound changes in apperception.[76]» In fact, the songs on *Kid A* feature bold, experimental arrangements and a rich sound that, if we think of the music scene of the late 1990s, can be even described as «avant-garde.» The song that is most representative of this search for a particular sound – achieved through the

---

73 Radiohead 2017, p. 136.
74 Radiohead 2017, p. 135.
75 Adorno 2016, p. 79.
76 Benjamin 2008, pp. 40-41.

abandonment of traditional song forms and the classic pop-rock sound that still lied at the base of *The Bends* and (a part of) *OK Computer*, in favor of engaging with electronic elements and computer techniques – is probably «Idioteque,» the eighth track of *Kid A*, composed entirely with non-traditional, technological, digital instruments. For Radiohead, «Idioteque» was the glorification of electronic music as well as an «attempt to capture the explosive rhythms of clubs[77]» (especially in light of Yorke's experiences as a DJ when he was a student), as it is entirely made up of electronic beats that repeat for the entire song, above which there is a twisting, four-notes melodic sequence inspired by «Mild und Leise,» one of Paul Lansky's electronic compositions.

«Idioteque» was considerably influenced by a certain genre of avant-garde pop music from the end of the 1990s, shown for example in the use of techniques from glitch music which creates unique sound effects through the intentional production of malfunctions and system errors of digital devices, like screeches, static, distortions, but also sudden melodic and rhythmic breaks. When inserted and integrated in the musical texture of a song, these sound effects shatter the listeners' expectations and the usual continuity of a song's development, yet they simultaneously acquire a unique meaning. These disturbing elements in glitch and ambient music become characteristic aspects and factors, like structural units that, along with traditional sounds, contribute to depicting a soundscape that is extended, discontinuous and fragmented. The pioneers of this genre (like Oval or, to mention a more popular artist, Björk) often made use of strategies like «draw[ing] lines on CDs with pens so as to get them to deliberately skip and glitch between pre-prepared tracks.[78]» During the compositional process of «Idioteque» Yorke also inserted an entire sample from a classical orchestra performance towards the end of the piece, thus creating a thundering wall of sound built with rock distortions and heterogeneous, eerie electronic sounds, at times even hypnotic, that confer to the song an atmosphere of «electronic esoterica.[79]»

77　Melissano 2003, p. 109.
78　Doheny 2002, p. 101.
79　Doheny 2002, p. 102.

The lyrics of the song are obscure and cryptic, with repeating, disjointed phrases, that almost seem to evoke a sort of «anxiously repeating "cut and paste" verses, telegraphing out their warnings.[80]» The listeners sometimes have the impression that the words and phrases used have been cut up and then randomly reassembled, which means that each time they take on a new, original subtlety of meaning based on how they are cut or how they are sung: «Who's in a bunker, who's in a bunker? / Women and children first, and the children first, and the children / I laugh until my head comes off, / I swallow 'til I burst, until I burst, until I...[81]» The voices are agitated, frenzied and – as they have been quite succinctly defined – «schizophrenic,[82]» perhaps in distress due to the imminent arrival of an apocalyptic situation, what is indicated throughout the song as the «Ice Age»: «Ice age coming, ice age coming, / Throw it in the fire, throw it in the fire, throw it on the...[83]» Precisely to what Yorke is referring to with this rather evocative image is *not* entirely clear. In this sense, and considering the lively interest in environmental issues shown by the band on multiple occasions, the allusion is probably a description of an age that, more so than any other in history, is the generator of the constant, rapid worsening of climate change and the arrival of the Anthropocene – i.e., «the period of time during which human activities have had an environmental impact on the Earth regarded as constituting a distinct geological age.[84]» Of course, in the context of the interpretation offered in this book, we can also conjecture that the «ice age» mentioned by Yorke is more generally a metaphor for the contemporary society, in an epoch in which every type of genuine relationship, true emotion and spontaneous action is apparently «frozen» by technologies that are used (or abused) to the extreme, as well as by the effects of a domineering and greedy economic system that renders humans powerless and paralyzes them, like statues of ice in front of the latest economic devices. Technology

---

80   Doheny 2002, p. 101.
81   Radiohead 2017, p. 140.
82   Melissano 2003, p. 110.
83   Radiohead 2017, p. 141.
84   Cited from: https://www.merriam-webster.com/dictionary/Anthropocene. For a recent philosophical critique of the concept of Anthropocene, see Friberg 2024.

and capitalist economy seem to be inextricably linked, which in turn is connected to the danger of extinction faced by every form of life, as shown by the lyrics: «We're not scaremongering, this is really happening, happening, / Mobile's working, mobile's chirping. / Take the money and run, take the money and run, take the money...[85]» However, the chorus of «Idioteque» seems to move away from the verse and the dystopian perspective it expresses, and it seems to offer an invocation or a sort of personal prayer, in other words the desire to save oneself from all of the disastrous things occurring in the world: «Here I'm allowed everything all of the time.[86]» In this regard, something particularly meaningful for the specific purposes of our argument here are the words Yorke recited at the end of the band's performance of the song at the Glastonbury festival in 2017: «Our children for our f***ing future – worth having – not one decided by useless politicians.[87]»

Beyond the avant-garde sounds created by technological means like samplers and digital softwares, on *Kid A* the band also manifested its interest in the first electronic instruments from the beginning of the 20th century: the Theremin and, even more so, its evolution, the ondes Martenot, the same instruments that various composers in the avant-garde movements of the 20th century showed enthusiasm for. In the case of Radiohead, it was Jonny Greenwood in particular that fell in love with the ondes Martenot – which he became familiar with through the compositions of Olivier Messiaen – causing it to be «the instrument for which he largely forsook the guitar on *Kid A*.[88]» The ondes Martenot is based on the same principles that regulate the function of the Theremin: sounds of various frequencies are created by the interfering in an invisible field of waves generated by two antennae with the hand; the creation of the sound does not involve any physical contact, with the only difference being that the instrument invented by Maurice Martenot is more intuitive than the Theremin because it is built like an analog instrument with a keyboard similar to that of a piano, which allows players to have traditional points of reference (the notes of the piano).

85　Radiohead 2017, p. 141.
86　Radiohead 2017, p. 140.
87　Oppenheim 2017.
88　Doheny 2002, p. 106.

The ondes Martenot appears in various tracks on *Kid A*: the most significant and easily perceived presence can be heard in «The National Anthem,» «How to Disappear Completely» and «Motion Picture Soundtrack.» «The National Anthem,» the third track of *Kid A*, is characterized by a wall of sound that imposingly invades the listening space, a mix of raging guitars, distortions and various background sounds from a variety of contexts, accompanied by an «insistent "funk" style drum beat.[89]» Indeed, in «The National Anthem» one can identify symphonies alternating with voices from the radio, newcasts, old films and other media: in brief, it can be considered a sort of «variety piece from the 1960s like Karlheinz Stockhausen's *Telemusik* or John Cage's works.[90]» Atop this vast, bizarre tapestry of sounds is the unmistakable timbre of the ondes Martenot, which seems to punctuate the unsettling, eerie effect that in some ways characterizes the mood of the whole album, alongside a section of wind instruments that appears towards the end of the song playing dissonant, out of tune notes, creating a climax that is resolved only with the song's conclusion (it is impossible to not think of «A Day in the Life» by The Beatles[91]).

«How to Disappear Completely,» the fourth track of *Kid A*, features the melancholic and distended sound of an acoustic guitar introduced by an initial cluster chord, the first chord of the song (reminiscent of Krzysztof Penderecki, Jonny Greenwood's favorite composer[92]), which seems to last for almost the entire length of the song, waiting in the background. This chord expresses a certain restlessness, miasma and instability that is described in the title of the song: «it is the sensation of a penultimate chord that is infinitely frozen, as if time was stopped in the moment before the final chord of a symphony.[93]» The otherworldly sound of the ondes Martenot appears towards the middle of the song, accentuating and increasing, once again, a feeling of individual detachment and alienation.

---

89   Solventi 2018, p. 151.
90   Solventi 2018, p. 93.
91   The centrality and the fundamental significance of experimentation in «A Day in the Life» for both the evolution of The Beatles and, more generally, the development of contemporary pop-rock music, has been aptly highlighted by Marco Maurizi (2019, p. 139).
92   Solventi 2018, p. 94.
93   Solventi 2018, p. 104.

«Motion Picture Soundtrack» is the final track of *Kid A* and sounds different, if compared to the rest of the album with its more technological, experimental and avant-garde style. This song, defined by its «antique style,[94]» indeed proves to be a more traditional composition in comparison to the rest of *Kid A*. «Motion Picture Soundtrack» is an unexpected and subdued dialogue, intimate and troubled, between the disheartened voice of the singer and the harmonium, as if it were a bare, disillusioned and humble lament. «The lush Disney-style jazz chordal cadences,» that shape the song's melody, may easily remind of «the lush songs and soundtracks of the classic 40s/50s Disney musicals,[95]» despite the lyrics that immediately move away from this type of fairytale imaginary: «Red wine and sleeping pills help me get back to your arms. / Cheap sex and sad films help me get where I belong.[96]» It is in the second chorus that, alongside the harp, the sound of the ondes Martenot slips into the song to proclaim lyrically and in an almost elegiac way its desolation, accompanied by the unique timbre of Thom Yorke's voice.

7.

The band's fifth album, *Amnesiac*, was born alongside *Kid A*, despite being subsequently released on the market. Indeed, the two projects are intimately linked and *Amnesiac* can be viewed as a continuation and a coherent development of *Kid A*, as there was «a kind of "symphonic" cohesion between tracks by having a small number of central lyrical themes.[97]» *Amnesiac* seems to be an echo, a reprisal and reinterpretation – still expressing a criticism of technology *through* a heavy-handed, intense use of technology – of *Kid A*, although almost all of the songs on the album are original compositions (besides «Morning Bell» and «Like Spinning Plates,» which are actually new interpretations and drafts of songs already included on *Kid A*). So, this album is also filled with technological

---

94   Melissano 2003, p. 112.
95   Doheny 2002, pp. 104, 107.
96   Radiohead 2017, p. 144.
97   Doheny 2002, p. 110.

sounds resulting from the band's search for a new style that has irreversibly marked its history and that, especially in this phase of its career, defined its aesthetics in a unique way. However, from a certain point of view *Amnesiac* also appears less daring and radical compared to the previous album, because the songs, as a whole, often have a more traditional form – and with this term we mean that they have a more analog sound, one that is produced by «real» musical instruments rather than by computers.[98]

Amnesiac has a unique, *sui generis* character. A musical material that is stylistically more composite, heterogeneous, but at the same time distinguished by a less cohesive, defined and solid aesthetics emerges, as if, in a certain sense, it had «the shape of the hesitation between two different clearly defined concepts.[99]» Of course, this almost mysterious configuration with its ambiguous stylistic peculiarity does *not* make the album less effective or vivid compared to *Kid A*. Indeed, *Amnesiac* has the power to fragment traditional musical language and rock itself through a critical adhesion to a view of technology as endowed with an expressive function. This fragmentation can be compared to the way in which the identities, ideals and values of the individuals are fragmented and liquefied in the heterogeneous context of the contemporary age: sense of direction, meanings, criteria, norms to orient oneself and choose the right path are all confused among the innumerable inputs and infinite amount of digital information that we are presented with today. The human being and technology seem to communicate without understanding each other, through interrupted signals that resonate in the ether, in search of a receiver that can hopefully capture these whispered messages and grasp their meaning, almost as if finding a «message in a bottle» – using an image quite dear to both Sting and Adorno,[100] who famously wrote in his *Philosophy of Modern Music*:

> The inhumanity of art must triumph over the inhumanity of the world for the sake of the humane. [...] The shocks of incomprehen-

---

98   For a general comment about the songs of *Amnesiac*, see Doheny 2002, pp. 108-129; Franchi 2009, pp. 252-292.
99   Solventi 2018, p. 158.
100 This is clearly a reference to the well known song «Message in a Bottle» by The Police. On this original juxtaposition of Adorno and Sting, see Früchtl 2019.

sion, emitted by artistic technique in the age of its meaninglessness, undergo a sudden change. They illuminate the meaningless world. Modern music sacrifices itself to this effort. It has taken upon itself all the darkness and guilt of the world. Its fortune lies in the perception of misfortune; all of its beauty is in denying itself the illusion of beauty. [...] Modern music sees absolute oblivion as its goal. It is the surviving message of despair from the shipwrecked.[101]

The songs included in *Amnesiac* are connected by the same common thread of meanings that characterized the songs of *Kid A*, but this album seems to arrive to the listener in a more enigmatic, irresolute manner, charged with a message that is subversive and visionary but fleeting, «usually more elusive than allusive.[102]» The same songs appear to orbit around a thematic cornerstone in a way that is freer, less defined, as if they were planets far from the center of the solar system, connected by a thin, flexible thread that weightlessly moves. «Pyramid Song,» the second track on *Amnesiac*, is characterized by an irregular, syncopated, almost unstable time signature, and unusual chord progressions built upon chords that create an atmosphere of tension and a dramatic intensity. It certainly *cannot* be considered a song with a regular, predictable or standardized form, but the arrangement, as a whole, is free of the compulsive beats and imposing technological filters that had characterized the style of many songs on Radiohead's previous album. It is primarily the unexpected entrance of the strings and harps that destabilizes and hypnotizes the listeners with the ethereal timbre of these instruments, aimed at endowing the piece with a sort of «exotic surface,[103]» an otherworldly and almost epic atmosphere. The digital sounds remain in the background and the ondes Martenot sound distant, discreet, whispered, as if to evoke the absurdity of a world in which technology and the subconscious melt together, without however reaching a clear sense of cohesion: certain fragments do not coincide, some parts do not perfectly dovetail together, the rhythm appears intentionally suspended and almost out of time (both literally and figuratively), out of sync with the

---

101   Adorno 2016, p. 94.
102   Solventi 2018, p. 161.
103   Solventi 2018, p. 160.

fundamental time signature of the piece, almost incomprehensible. Thom Yorke's voice and the piano are the cornerstone of the song, as if he were the last man on earth singing his dissonant, disoriented song with this forgotten instrument: «Jumped in the river and what did I see? / Black-eyed angels swam with me. / [...] All my lovers were there with me, / All my past and futures.[104]»

«Knives Out,» the sixth track of the album, is the song on *Amnesiac* that apparently maintains a more traditional structure and sound compared to the rest of the record. It can be considered as «the counterpart to "Optimistic" [on *Kid A*],[105]» which was also the sixth track of its album, while in terms of its lyrics and music, it evokes «the quasi-baroque "rain down" section of "Paranoid Android".[106]» The melody is based on magnetic, refined, «spiraling[107]» chord progressions from the guitar that constantly repeat throughout the song, becoming «gently head-spinning» and having a «disorientating effect[108]» at times, creating an auditory background for lyrics that are rather distressing and disoriented, full of almost horrific images: «So knives out, catch the mouse, don't look down, shove it in your mouth. [...] / So knives out, cook him up, squash his head, put him in the pot.[109]»

Amnesiac, even more so than *Kid A* in certain ways, develops the aesthetics that Radiohead arrived at in the second phase of its evolution, in part through the echo of a significant, tangible jazz influence that can be heard in the songs' articulated rhythms (that often blossom into full-fledged polyrhythms) and the vaguely modal, composite harmonies. After all, Yorke mentioned multiple times that he had been inspired by the music of jazz players such as Charles Mingus and Alice Coltrane during the composition of many songs on *Amnesiac*, like «Pyramid Song.» These echoes of jazz and blues are constantly reworked and woven together with the band's synthetic sound in an intentionally enigmatic and paradoxical manner, to the point where they (seemingly) disappear under carpets of digital sound: in this context, there is no longer space for a fully coherent

---

104   Radiohead 2017, p. 152.
105   Solventi 2018, p. 162.
106   Doheny 2002, p. 122.
107   Solventi 2018, p. 162
108   Doheny 2002, p. 122.
109   Radiohead 2017, p. 159.

and culturally unifying imaginary like in the past, at least not in the way that it had traditionally been understood. Radiohead makes use of jazz but deforms it, almost aping it, like in the last song of the album, «Life In a Glasshouse,» that in a certain sense «cynically» closes the album. Indeed, the song is performed by a jazz band so out of tune that it seems tragicomic, as if it were at a carnival or a funeral, «led by British "trad" jazz legend Humphrey Lyttelton.[110]» Yorke's slightly off-key voice, engaging in a call and response with the strident high notes of the winds, seems particularly effective and touching precisely because of this dissonance. In brief, *Amnesiac* apparently shows a desire to find a greater balance between digital and analog sounds: the latter resurface with greater force, increased lyricism and drama, compared to *Kid A*, nonetheless developing in directions that are just as intriguing and provoking. Here past and future, tradition and innovation are able to harmonize, through invisible melodic lines, with imaginary visions and evocative symbols. *Amnesiac*, by association, «[is] about... the things you forget. And remembering.[111]»

According to his unique ontological conception of technology, basically presented in his famous essay *The Question Concerning Technology*, Heidegger states that «[t]he "essence of *Technik* is by no means anything technological." [...] Technology is not primarily a way of making or doing things, but a way of revealing things that precedes the making,[112]» that is, a dimension that emerges in the domain in which truth (originally understood by Heidegger as *alētheia*, i.e. «unconcealment») comes to presence and happens. «How should we respond to technology? Not by a flight into mysticism, superstition and irrationalism,» for Heidegger, inasmuch as «these are an essential adjunct of technological rationalism.» Rather, for Heidegger «[w]e should reflect on beings» and, in particular, «reflect on the essence of *Technik*, "the remedy that grows where the danger is" (Hölderlin), for this is related to *Technik,* yet not itself technological and will lead us to think about art.[113]» Heidegger's conception of technology, strictly

---

110 Doheny 2002, p. 129.
111 Yorke, cited in Doheny 2002, p. 111.
112 Inwood 1999, 209-210.
113 Inwood 1999, 211-212.

tied to fundamental philosophical themes such as the history of metaphysics, the «oblivion of Being» and nihilism,[114] is too broad and complex to be fully examined in the specific context of an investigation of the relation between music and technology with a precise and delimited focus on Radiohead. Put simply, in the limits of that which is fruitful for our investigation, the idea is that, from this perspective, it is only in and through technology – which has become ineradicable, because it has fulfilled its destiny and has become an essential component of modernity – that certain hints and signals can be intuited and perceived, with which one can attempt to interpret the contemporary age and understand its truth (and, dialectically, at the same time also its untruth). As far as how bold a connection between a philosophy like Heidegger's and a music like Radiohead's regarding these themes truly seems, we believe that works (and, indeed, masterworks) like *Kid A* and *Amnesiac* draw closer to this perspective, opening an original dimension in the musical horizon of Radiohead and pushing the band towards the beginning of a new phase in its unique aesthetics.

---

114   «After *Being and Time* (1927)» for Heidegger «technology becomes the hidden destiny of modern metaphysics. [...] And therefore what is now thinking? Or rather: is it still possible to think after metaphysics is fulfilled as the world of technology? [...] [The] question of being becomes now the interrogation of the destiny of technology. Human existence is involved in this destiny [...]. This is how the technological humans live, confident, in the endlessness of the void of their own finitude. [...] In this sense, we can begin to understand that *technology is nihilism* in its deepest sense, what Heidegger interprets [...] as the *Not der Notlosigkeit*, the condition of extreme distress experienced by those who do not recognize their own distress» (Ruggenini 2002, pp. 225, 228, 235).

CHAPTER THREE
REGAINING THE SOUL
THROUGH TECHNOLOGY
From *Hail to the Thief* to *A Moon Shaped Pool*

1.

Reflections on the role art plays in society are multifaceted and complex, and they often require an investigation of the relationship that an artwork establishes with its historical and cultural context, as well as the results of this relationship, creating spaces for discussion characterized by diverse and at times dissenting opinions. Every work of art, just like every specific artistic movement, is affected by the influences and the constraints of its original historical context in a complex relationship of interdependence. The forms, languages, contents and styles used by a certain artist or a certain artistic movement *cannot* be separated from the context and society in which they operate; they are formed as reactions to (and interactions with) that society, although *without* establishing a one-sided and deterministic relationship, given that the effects and outcomes of this relationship are often unpredictable and variable.

This debate leads us to the fundamental question of whether or not a work of art can be considered a mere product or a simple consequence of a certain historical, economic, political and cultural context – thus denying its autonomy and individuality – or if, conversely, it should be considered an entity endowed with at least a certain degree of freedom regarding its context. According to the latter viewpoint, a work of art is capable to capture, transfigure and bring to expression the latent meanings, manifestations and tendencies of its context in a unique manner. As it is relevant for the purposes of the cohesiveness of the argument presented in this book, we consider it useful to refer again to Theodor W. Adorno, the famous Frankfurt philosopher, sociologist and musicologist, whose thinking is able to identify the complexities and even the antinomies of the existing reality.

As is well known, Adorno does not consider art as a fully autonomous object, nor, vice-versa, as an artifact that is entirely dependent on its social context, rather a dialectical product that is twofold and actually has a «double character as both autonomous and *fait social*.[1]» As Adorno explains, «[t]he double character of art – something that severs itself from empirical reality and thereby from society's functional context and yet is at the same time part of empirical reality and society's functional context – is directly apparent in the aesthetic phenomena, which are both aesthetic and *faits sociaux*.[2]» In other words, for Adorno, in light of an examination of the relationship between art and society, art should be considered dialectically as both a social fact, which is to say tied to the circumstances of its time, and an autonomous fact, i.e. a product that claims an independent legitimacy and significance. What Adorno precisely identifies as a degree of partial detachment from reality (and, therefore, independence and freedom from it) is a necessary condition for art to be able reveal the instabilities and disharmonies of the present age, in a world that the German philosopher considers distorted and untrue.[3] For example, «[t]he basis of the isolation of radical modern music,» according to Adorno, «is not its asocial, but precisely its social substance.[4]» For this reason, through an Adornian lens, true art is provided with an epistemological value, i.e. a «truth content (*Wahrheitsgehalt*),» when it induces in its audience a knowledge of «what is» through its negation; for Adorno, this is art's «great refusal» of leisure and entertainment as its ultimate ends (especially in relation to the issues regarding the culture industry and popular music), or the refusal of soothing melodies and harmonies as means of entertainment and therefore as a way to (falsely) reconcile with reality.

As per the music of Radiohead, it is undeniable how much of the band's production can at times seem less than «pleasant» upon first listen, and at times even arcane, difficult, hermetic and exoteric. Because of the peculiar and complex musical language developed through the band's tireless artistic exploration, this

---

1   Adorno 2002a, p. 5.
2   Adorno 2002a, p. 252.
3   On this topic, see Marino 2019.
4   Adorno 2016, p. 92.

(positively, i.e. aesthetically fascinating) «unpleasant» quality became noticeable particularly after the band decided to dedicate itself to technological experimentation in order to better express its critique of contemporary society. Especially the musical style of the second phase of the band's career rarely seems to subscribe to the standard, canonical forms of commercial and mainstream pop-rock music.

In order to once again establish a connection between Adorno's philosophy and Radiohead's music – precisely because the latter does *not* pander to the listeners' standardized expectations, but instead attempts to find an aesthetic form that critically challenges the real through technological innovations and artificial sounds –, we can say that the English band seems to move towards a kind of music that is authentic because of its critical nature, precisely what Adorno exalted in his conception of the work of art. Although Radiohead has never identified with the traditional idea of the socially and politically committed pop-rock band, and despite the fact that after the success of «Creep» (the band's first hit single) Radiohead was not confined to the category of underground bands, but experienced a level of popularity comparable to mainstream musicians, it is nevertheless undeniable how, through an unceasing process of experimentation, the music of Radiohead has taken on (in an Adornian way, so to speak) the character of works of art that adopt a critical position on the existing reality, pierce the veil that masks the social contradictions in which ideologies lie, and, in this way, reveal the prospect of a possible, utopian reconciliation in the future. From this point of view, in reference to a recent interpretation of the various phenomena that populate the universe of current pop-rock music, one could probably place Radiohead within the realm of the so-called «alternative mainstream» genre.[5]

---

5   This category refers to the interesting analysis carried out by Parapar 2021 (p. 195), that, making use of Gert Keunen's categorization, writes: «there exist musical works within the culture industry which afford critical abstraction, to act negatively and to grant a space of freedom (here resides the critical force of reason). On this point, Gert Keunen talks about "pop mainstream," "underground," and "alternative mainstream." According to this division, we consider that the first category would contribute to identity thinking, the second would collaborate in critical thinking, and the

2.

Keeping these preliminary remarks in mind as we return to our interpretation of the «philosophy of Radiohead,» articulated according to the chronological release of their albums, we can say that *Hail to the Thief* (2003) appears to be the band's most actively «antagonistic[6]» work regarding its social context.[7] It is through this character, so clearly visible on *Hail to the Thief*, that Radiohead abandons the feelings of despair and detachment regarding reality that in some ways had characterized the band's previous work. In its sixth album, the band appears openly engaged in a critical dialogue with sociopolitical topics for the first time, one led by a deep, strong desire to assume responsibility regarding the political and cultural situation at the time and an authentic «search for truth,[8]» a desire to demystify social illusions through free, autonomous music.[9] Yet the political engagement present on the album *never* suffocates the band's aesthetics, anything but: despite discussing themes related to current affairs, the lyrics of *Hail to the Thief* never slip into the realm of propaganda or explicit protest (like what happened in the lyrics of many of its contemporaries), but actually maintain the level of allusiveness and implicitness that have always characterized the aesthetics of the band. A large part of the lyrics of *Hail to the Thief* were developed through a composite cut-up technique, «an increasingly complex game of textual maneuvers and allusions,[10]» which ensures that each song's musical aspect, on the one hand, and the expression of an individual point of view deeply critical of the dominant social system, on the other, prevail. In any case, the political commentary, although never entirely obvious, is nonetheless visible, even in the title of the album

---

third, being a hybrid between pop mainstream and underground, could contribute to either of the two.»

6   Solventi 2018, p. 197.
7   For a general comment about the songs of *Hail to the Thief*, see Franchi 2009, pp. 294-357.
8   Solventi 2018, pp. 197-198.
9   On the relation between music and politics in Radiohead's unique aesthetics, with a particular focus on *Hail to the Thief*, see the essays included in the fourth part of Forbes and Reisch 2009 (Lougheed 2009; Melançon 2009; Burt 2009; Forbes 2009; Lee 2009).
10   Solventi 2018, p. 190.

itself, making use of the provocative chant («Hail to the thief, our commander in chief[11]») that crowds of protestors shouted in the US capital following George W. Bush's inauguration as president of the United States.

The topics discussed in the lyrics of *Hail to the Thief* find their match on the formal level in the album's music, which proves to be a composite «musical compilation[12]» in which disparate (or even quite conflicting) genres, styles and themes find a meaningful synthesis. The first sound of the album that the listener encounters is the audible electric vibration produced the moment the jack of the guitar is inserted into the amp, which immediately communicates the general aims of the album: namely, the desire to return to a musical arrangement that is in part more conventional, closer to the canonical auditory realm of a pop-rock band that mainly uses traditional instruments (like electric guitars). Indeed, the recording process, which mostly occurred at Ocean Way Recording Studios in Los Angeles – an unusual location for a band like Radiohead, who had previously recorded in more secluded and decidedly less trendy locations[13] –, was apparently dominated by a more spontaneous, impulsive creative approach to musical composition. In fact, it seems that in the early stages of the process the band decided to fully abandon digital instruments in an attempt to capture the essence of what makes a song «good» (and therefore musically significant), without covering up this essence through an excessive use of digital effects in the post-production process.[14]

---

11 See https://citizeninsane.eu/media/ita/jam/pt_2003-06_jam.htm.

12 Solventi 2018, p. 194.

13 Thom Yorke described the experience during an interview as follows: «It was sort of like holiday camp. We went to a couple of glamorous parties, which really helped. We don't have enough glamour in our lives. Too much news radio, not enough glamour» (Frickle 2003).

14 Once again, we would like to refer to Thom Yorke's own statements on the experience of recording *Hail to the Thief*: «The last two studio records [*Kid A* and *Amnesiac*] were a real headache. We had spent so much time looking at computers and grids, we were like, "That's enough. We can't do that anymore." This time, we used computers, but they had to actually be in the room with all the gear. So everything was about performance, like staging a play» (cited from: https://web.archive.org/web/20071020161123/http://mtv.com/bands/r/Radiohead/news_feature_061903/index2.jhtml).

At this point, it comes quite naturally to return to the triadic scheme that lies at the base of our interpretive framework: the idea that Radiohead's musical production, as a whole, can be divided into three moments or phases, according to the relationship that the band establishes with technology, both in relation to the thematic content of the songs and their explicitly musical and formal qualities. From this point of view, *Hail to the Thief* undoubtedly marks the end of what we consider the second stage of the band's musical production and ushers in the subsequent third stage. According to our interpretation, this third stage is characterized by the moment in which Radiohead's music aims to create a synthesis – and therefore a sort of reconciliation – with technology, inaugurating a new aesthetics marked by a return to the expressive and subjective level, and by a musical vision that is no longer «technocentric,» so to speak, but «anthropocentric.» This shifts the focus to the expression of a subjective human experience that becomes the thematic center of the band's creations and therefore defines the aspirations motivating the musical compositions, while the digital dimension becomes a tool that is able to render the band's language more relevant and effective. In summary, despite the fact that a strong proclivity for radical experimentation with technological sounds that had characterized the band's previous albums (*Kid A, Amnesiac*) is abandoned in this third phase, electronic elements still play a prominent role in the band's work, in support of the expressive needs of the main narrating voice. Therefore, from *Hail to the Thief* to *A Moon Shaped Pool*, it is the voice of the individual that returns to a position of priority and reacquires its primacy, which is confirmed by the lyrics (it is no coincidence that they feature more introspective contents, related to human fragility and vulnerability), as well as by the melodies (that are often more singable and sometimes expressed through a more traditional instrumentation), contrary to the previous two albums that we have placed within the second phase of Radiohead's musical aesthetics and that, as we have shown, were characterized by the cerebral, obscure and at times impenetrable technological density of the band's music.

Therefore, in the rather eclectic and composite auditory dimension of *Hail to the Thief*, «heavy techno rhythms [...] and refined, pristine passages inspired by jazz and blues[15]» find a space in which they can open a dialogue: analog instruments alongside synthesizers, digital audio software, drum machines and the already familiar ondes Martenot have a greater impact through this union, in which technology, even when it aggressively enters the sound texture, still appears with the aim of underpinning the main message of the song, thus increasing its expressive effectiveness and power. From the point of view of the themes and contents of the album, *Hail to the Thief* is «permeated by a mystical, fantastical dimension,[16]» inspired by characters from cartoons, children's tales (there are references to the animated film *Chicken Little*, or the story of Aladdin), as well as literature and religious myth (the story of Noah and the Ark in the song «Sail to the Moon,» for example), with the purpose of tackling thorny, topical themes from original perspectives, like «the fact of choosing whether to ignore or not what was happening in the world.[17]» Every song of *Hail to the Thief* is accompanied by a subtitle that alludes to the different references each song is linked to or was inspired by.

According to some statements of the band's members, many songs on *Hail to the Thief* were the result of Thom Yorke's vocal improvisations that he came up with during his long, aimless drives that he often took in the countryside near his home around sunset. It is this vague atmosphere, enveloped in a crepuscular, dusky light, that becomes an objective counterpart of the restlessness regarding the current state of the world, firmly expressed by many songs on this album. This dimension, suspended in a sort of absurd eternity on the boundary separating day and night (in some ways a prelude and metaphor for a transition whose outcome is yet to be revealed), metaphorically alludes to the inevitable and uncontrollable sociopolitical changes occurring in the world, against which the individuals often feel powerless.

«The Gloaming,» the eighth track on the album and «its heart and center of gravity,[18]» encapsulates the profound meaning of

---

15   Melissano 2003, p. 140.
16   Melissano 2003, p. 140.
17   Melissano 2003, p. 139.
18   Solventi 2018, p. 195.

Hail to the Thief as it expresses this sensation of anticipation, filled with hope and, simultaneously, anxiety, represented by the touching image of a rural landscape in the twilight.[19] The piece is entirely constructed with an electronic base composed by overlapping and seemingly out-of-rhythm loops, with rather enigmatic, evocative lyrics consisting of short, fragmented, repeating phrases – developed using the cut-up technique – that aid in recreating a dreamlike atmosphere that conjures up the feeling of uneasiness that the title alludes to: a dimension of darkness that slowly seems to envelop and surround the entire humankind. It is easy to lose contact with reality and rationality in the shadows, moving blindly forward in the throes of fear of the unknown, passively abandoning oneself to the course of events, as if in a hypnotic state of numbness. The song intones: «Genie let out of the bottle, it is now the witching hour / Murderers you're murderers, we are not the same as you,[20]» and then continues: «They will suck you down, to the otherside / To the shadows blue & red [...] / Your alarm bells, your alarm... / They should be ringing.[21]»

Moving backwards to the opening track of *Hail to the Thief*, we can say that the song «2+2=5[22]» expresses from the very beginning an impulsive, vital energy that serves as the base of the entire album. The powerful contrasts between the verses and the refrains

---

19   «The band's original title for the album was *The Gloaming*, which, Greenwood explains, "is an old English word for that period of half light before it becomes dark. The world feels a bit like that at the moment." The group felt that *The Gloaming* sounded "too prog-rock," however, so that became the album's subtitle» (KRT 2003).
20   Radiohead 2017, p. 192.
21   Radiohead 2017, p. 193.
22   As Yorke explained about the subtitle of the song: «The lukewarm is something from Dante. If I remember this rightly, it's the least nasty bit of hell, just as you walk through the door there're the "Lukewarm." And the lukewarm hang around and they were never really bothered about, they didn't believe in anything particularly. They were like, "Oh, you know, whatever, there's nothing I can do about it. No, no, no." And it's quite a curious thing that Dante presents you with. All of a sudden you have these people and you think, "Well, they haven't really done anything wrong, they just didn't do anything." And so he judges them and puts them there which, I think, is actually a really good way of explaining "2+2=5".» (cited from: https:// citizeninsane.eu/music/httt/2plus2is5.html).

(in which the former, upon a fascinating 7/8 time signature, are contrasted with an explosive refrain) present the listener with an imposing wall of sound created through significant auditory contrasts. After the first opening verses and their moderate tempo, the chorus erupts into an «a sudden burst of flaming guitars,[23]» creating a general sense of tension in the listener like a «jolt of electricity.[24]» The contrast does not lie only in the particular use of the musical dynamics, but also in the simultaneous, powerful presence of analog and technological instruments together, that play together with the shared goal of emphasizing the urgency of the message and the state of mind expressed in the lyrics, exemplified in the chorus that, as if it were a reproach, calls out, enraged: «You have not been paying attention.[25]» The subtitle of the song, «The Lukewarm,» seems to be inspired by the «Canto III» of Dante Alighieri's *Hell*, and refers to those who, lacking judgment, decided to live without infamy and at the same time without praise, in a sort of condition of apathy and indifference both to good and evil.[26]

The second track of *Hail to the Thief*, «Sit Down. Stand Up,» drips with technological sounds. The vocal melody, accompanied by the piano, rests atop a base created by looping digital pulses that towards the middle of the song – together with drummer Phil Selway's throbbing rhythm – explode into a soundscape that has echoes of jungle and drum & bass styles, while Yorke's voice obsessively repeats the words «The raindrops.[27]» The lyrics once again describe a hellish, almost Dantean landscape, for example: «Walk into the jaws of hell, [Sit down], walk into the jaws of hell [Stand up],[28]» where the rain might recall «the eternal,

---

23   Solventi 2018, p. 186.
24   Solventi 2018, p. 186.
25   Radiohead 2017, p. 179.
26   As Virgil explains to Dante at the gates of hell, at the beginning of the «Canto III» of *Hell*: «This miserable fate / Suffer the wretched souls of those who lived / Without or praise or blame, with that ill band / Of angels mix'd, who nor rebellious proved, / Nor yet were true to God, but for themselves / Were only. [...] Fame of them the world hath none, / Nor suffers; mercy and justice scorn them both. Speak not of them, but look, and pass them by» (Alighieri 1982, p. 24).
27   Radiohead 2017, p. 181.
28   Radiohead 2017, p. 180.

accursed, cold, and heavy rain» that tortures the damned in the Third Circle of Dante's *Hell* (that of the gluttonous), making them «howl like dogs».[29]

«Sail to the Moon,» the third track of *Hail to the Thief*, is a touching ballad, introduced by melancholic, jazz-inspired chords played almost exclusively by the piano. The dreamlike atmosphere of «Sail to the Moon» vaguely brings to mind «Pyramid Song,» with which it shares its challenging time signature and references to a cosmic imaginary («A moon full of stars and astral cars,[30]» from the song on *Amnesiac*). Despite the sluggish pace of the song and the almost plaintive nature of Yorke's voice, this song is considered by the singer to be a «a love letter» filled with hope for his son Noah, as it focuses on the biblical figure of Noah and the salvation offered by his ark. Looking at each of the songs on *Hail to the Thief*, it becomes clear how the more traditional compositions, marked by sounds produced by analog instruments rather than electronic and digital instruments, alternate with more experimental, technological pieces, as if their position in the tracklist was ruled by a set of precise, predetermined criteria. With this consideration, we would like to underline that, once again, the fundamental features of the peculiar, distinctive language used by Radiohead *cannot* be assimilated into a rigid categorization; rather, they are subject to a continuous formal reworking «on the level of a synthesis between the analog and the digital dimensions,[31]» and therefore oscillating between the human and the machine.

---

29   Alighieri 1952, p. 8. In the «Canto VI» of *Hell* Dante finds himself in the Third Circle, where he observes the gluttonous' torment, which is «to lie in the mire, under a continual and heavy storm of hail, snow, and discoloured water; Cerberus meanwhile barking over them with his threefold throat, and rending them piecemeal» (Alighieri 1982, p. 42). As Dante himself writes in this part of *The Divine Comedy*: «In the third circle I arrive, of showers / Ceaseless, accursed, heavy and cold, unchanged / For ever, both in kind and in degree. Large hail, discolour'd water, sleety flaw / Through the dun midnight air stream'd down amain: / Stank all the land whereon that tempest fell. [...] / We, o'er the shades thrown prostrate by the brunt / Of the heavy tempest passing, set our feet / Upon their emptiness, that substance seem'd» (Alighieri 1982, p. 42).
30   Radiohead 2017, p. 152.
31   Solventi 2018, p. 190.

3.

At this point in our discussion, it can be interesting to draw another connection between some eminent thinkers of the 20th century – precisely those who felt the need to face the pressing theme of modernity embodied by technological progresses – with the goal of broadening the scope of our discourse on Radiohead's music and finding more comprehensive meanings in the band's musical production. Following long, profound reflections on society and technological development in the first half of the 20th century, some philosophers defined an ideal ethics for modern humans in the face of their contemporary context, as well as the most fitting attitude towards this technologized reality: an attitude intended to, in essence, «preserve technology» in order to «overcome it.[32]» In other words, several thinkers from the 20th century understood the ineffectiveness of individual resistance against an increasing evolved daily life dominated by an ideology in favor of technology, or even «technocentric,» that seems to prefer a utopia (or dystopia, depending on our point of view) of simple technological progress compared to one characterized by authentic human development. Various 20th-century thinkers suggested that human beings' recovery of selfhood was possible by first starting with an awareness and knowledge of the operational mechanisms that lie behind technology. Through acceptance rather than refusal it is possible to counteract the domination of technology and reestablish the centrality of human beings, according to a vision that sees the overcoming of that which is cold and distant from human sensibility (technology) as revealing a deeper awareness that enables a meditation on the «absolute presence» of the human being in the world, which is to say a «freedom that is greater than every material object.[33]» The idea that «technological rationalization offers human beings a greater possibility of being present in reflection, and ultimately renders them more free,[34]» ultimately finds an application and coherence if placed in relation to Radiohead's musical trajectory and, more

---

32   Nacci 2000, p. 99.
33   Nacci 2000, p. 99 (with specific reference to Jaspers).
34   Nacci 2000, pp. 99-100.

specifically, the many songs that we have placed within the third phase of the band's artistic production discussed in this chapter.

To this end, the band's next album, *In Rainbows*, compared to the previous works, puts greater emphasis on the expressive and purely human component of the songs. In particular, *In Rainbows* emphasizes the psychological and existential introspective gaze of the individuals, supported by the band's use of a technological syntax developed throughout the years. This occurs first and foremost in the lyrics of the songs on *In Rainbows*.[35] In *Hail to the Thief*, the narrator's gaze was projected toward an outward warring social dimension, and therefore often addressed an external individual, sometimes through the use of the personal pronoun «you» with confrontational and exhortatory tones, as if to call the listener's attention to the difficult global situation. In this regard, it is useful to recall certain cutting, accusatory and at times sarcastic lyrics from «2+2=5,» for example: «Are you such a dreamer? To put the world to rights?[36]»; or lyrics from «We Suck Young Blood»: «Are you fracturing? Are you torn at the seams? / Would you do anything? / Flea-bitten? Moth-eaten? / We suck young blood.[37]»

However, on *In Rainbows* the narrator tends to play the role of an introspective first-person protagonist focused on his own private circumstances. The lyrics of «House of Cards» reflect this psychological dimension that flows throughout the album and present the protagonist's inner dynamics: «I don't want to be your friend, I just want to be your lover. / No matter how it ends, no matter how it starts. / Forget about your house of cards and I'll do mine.[38]» The poetic image of the house of cards evoked in the lyrics alludes to a fragile, delicate structure, exposed to the harsh outer world and its events: even a gentle breeze can threaten such a precarious construction, something that the time and care required in upholding cannot cope with. This image can be understood as a metaphor for the fragility and vulnerability of human relationships, and their exposure to the inevitable randomness

---

35   For a general comment about the songs of *In Rainbows*, see Franchi 2009, pp. 360-406.
36   Radiohead 2017, p. 178.
37   Radiohead 2017, pp. 190-191.
38   Radiohead 2017, p. 234.

and the volatile misfortunes that may always characterize human life, and how the commitment and dedication required in building these relationships are rarely counterbalanced by a guarantee of security or the promise of stability over time. The initial guitar riff is imbued with a strange nostalgic atmosphere that permeates the entire song and that, paired with Thom Yorke's delicate vocalizations, creates a languid, satiny atmosphere of «a kind of lunar soul music,[39]» rich with reverberations and intimate, almost spiritual energies, in which the narrator's unique existential condition expressed in the lyrics is projected in a broader and, in some ways, even universal collective dimension.

Every composition on *In Rainbows* highlights an antinomical nucleus that oscillates between traditional and synthetic/digital sounds, although the recovery of a certain musical enjoyment stands as the record's premise and its ultimate end. In this regard, in his book *Rocksofia* Alessandro Alfieri has examined the conceptual pair of «originality in musical construction and sound,» on the one side, and the «enjoyable, fascinating and poetic melodies,[40]» on the other, identifying it as the veritable essence of the original musical language developed by Radiohead as a reaction to the widespread generational uneasiness and discontent of the late 1990s. This distress and discomfort pushed many other contemporary bands (whose destinies were certainly much less fortunate and enduring compared to Radiohead) to develop an aesthetics overly tied to musical trends and styles that were outdated or marked by a «manic emphasis on the aspect of existential depression of younger generations unaffected by political passions,» or by the worship of «technical intellectualism» and the triumph of the «ostentatious display of musical virtuosity.[41]»

In *In Rainbows* it is therefore the technological dimension – comprising digital samplers, computerized sounds, beats from drum machines, and so on – that is in contrast with a greater singability, achieved through refined, seductive harmonies and dense, sophisticated melodies, embodied in Thom York's soft falsetto, particularly important in songs like «Nude» and «Reckoner.» «All

---

39   Solventi 2018, p. 228.
40   Alfieri 2019, p. 69.
41   Alfieri 2019, pp. 69-70.

I Need,» the album's fifth track, includes a simple instrumentation – primarily a distorted electric bass and drums – that, however, is able to define a captivating melodic motif that creates an overall atmosphere that is intriguing and mysterious, in which Yorke's dark lament rises up: «I'm an animal trapped in your hot car. / I am all the days that you choose to ignore. / You are all I need.[42]»

The themes that lie at the base of *In Rainbows*, the unifying sensibility, style and mood that pull the songs together, remain rather vague and abstract, ascribable, if anything, to the inner, psychological sphere that characterizes each song. In the few, laconic public statements given for the release of *In Rainbows*, Thom Yorke offered some approximate information on the origin and sources of inspiration behind the album. During an interview, in response to a question on the type of individual discomfort and malaise that seemed to emanate from the album's lyrics, Yorke quite spontaneously replied that they were the result of «the fucking panic of realising you're going to die» and the sensation that «any time soon [I could] possibly [have] a heart attack when I next go for a run.[43]»

In this sense, the most important song (in terms of content) of the entire album is probably the striking, poetic, ethereal and somehow transcendental «Reckoner.» In fact, it is precisely in the central verses of this song that the foundational intuition that the rest of *In Rainbows* lies on can be found: «Dedicated to all hu... all human beings / Because we separate like ripples on a blank shore[44]» («In rainbows»). It is interesting to reflect on the title of the song. Indeed, the term itself, «reckoner,» is ambiguous: if, in various contexts, this word can be understood as meaning «calculator» or «device for calculating,» in this song it could also mean «he/she who calculates» or «he/she who evaluates and judges,» i.e., it is not entirely clear whether Yorke in the song is having a conversation with a computer, a robot, or a particularly calculating human being[45] – for example, one who embodies what Heidegger critically called «*das rechnende Denken*, "calculating thinking," or *das Rechnen*, "reckoning, calculation," from

---

42   Radiohead 2017, p. 228.
43   McLean 2007.
44   Radiohead 2017, p. 232.
45   Franchi 2009, pp. 388-389.

rechnen, "to reckon, etc.," a word that, together with compounds such as *berechnen*, "to calculate," usually conveys Heidegger's disapproval,» as opposed to what he considered instead «genuine philosophical thinking.[46]» In an attempt to discern connections between the aforementioned song and the central role played by the theme of technology in the context of this book, it seems that even in the ambiguous meaning of the title «Reckoner» the indelible duplicity that we have examined so far once again becomes clear: namely, the antinomical pair that identifies a contraposition of (and, indeed, a dialectical relationship between) terms like humanity/technology and analog/digital.

«Reckoner» is a ballad essentially comprising a refined, minimal melody, an arpeggio played by the guitar that is repeated for almost the entire length of the song, and a vital rhythmic texture (formed by various percussion instruments like the drums and tambourines) which gives the song an overall sensation of a dynamic, insistent and untiring whirlwind. Yorke's falsetto, used for the whole song, and the melodic motif of the guitar seem to come together in a profound, enveloping and captivating fusion, until the central section of «Reckoner» (that is also the most important part of the song) in which these two elements step back to give space to the sound of a captivating string ensemble arranged by Jonny Greenwood. Ultimately, towards the end of the song, the sound of the string instruments interlaces with Yorke's voice and the original guitar motif into a dense and touching harmonic texture, like different overlapping levels of sound that are refracted into and through each other «like ripples on a blank shore.[47]»

As we said, there are various references to the theme of technology scattered throughout *In Rainbows*, even if they are not always explicit or denoted by digital sounds and electronic experimentations. At times these references are indeed cultural, mentions of specific instrumental performance techniques or figures and characters that were proponents of artistic innovations related to technological revolutions in music. Let us simply think of the song «Faust Arp,» whose title alone (as well as the similarities in the style of the guitar and the melody) is connected

---

46   Inwood 1999, p. 216.
47   Radiohead 2017, p. 232.

to the first bars of the composition «Läuft... Heißt Das Es Läuft Oder Es Kommt Bald... Läuft» from the album *Faust IV* by Faust, an important group part of the *Krautrock* music scene in Germany in the 1970s. The term *Krautrock* famously refers to a musical style in popular music characterized by a strong element of electronic experimentalism in the sound of various bands belonging to this movement, on the heels of the epic experiences of composers of electro-acoustic music and *musique concrète* in the previous years, especially those of the German composer Karlheinz Stockhausen.

In conclusion, with *In Rainbows* Radiohead seemed to define, once again quite effectively, its peculiar expressive language, as well as its remarkable ability, as a band, to explore a wide variety of complex and multiple auditory universes. Due to the poignancy of the contents and the elegance of the sound, this album underlines the band's unique position within the pop-rock landscape at the beginning of the 21st century – a topic that will be further discussed in the final chapter of this book. At the same time, precisely because of the commitment and involvement required during this creative phase, *In Rainbows* marked a very important chapter in the musical trajectory of the band. In the years that followed, Radiohead introduced other changes in its artistic approach, in search of new forms of expression and a renewed creative authenticity in an effort to maintain the enthusiasm, spontaneity and energy required to *not* fall back into «already-heard» or «pre-digested» musical styles.

4.

Four years after the release of *In Rainbows*, the band released the album *The King of Limbs* in 2011, disorienting its fans by adopting a partially new style. *The King of Limbs* is characterized by a new deep journey into the obscure depths of the universe of computers and electronic sounds. In some ways, the aesthetic profile of *The King of Limbs* may recall the artistic journey of *Kid A* and *Amnesiac*, but an attentive listening reveals how different these works really are. In other words, *The King of Limbs*, contrary to what a superficial listen of the album's sound would suggest, plants its roots in the (pre-technological, so to speak) theme of nature. This leitmotif accompanies and more or less palpably distinguishes each song on the album, both in terms of contents (note how each song has a title that alludes to the earthly dimension of the natural world, including the title of the album itself) and metaphorically – as we will discuss in greater detail – in terms of the album's sound.

The natural dimension at the center of this album is not only related to the theme of the environment or, more specifically, the theme of humans respecting (or disrespecting) the earth – a theme that is incidentally very dear to the band. Rather, this dimension also includes broad nuances in meaning related to nature, like the primordial universe of natural impulses and human urges that are sometimes out of the control of our rational understanding and reflective judgment. Keeping this in mind, the origins and reasons behind the obscure and overall enigmatic nature of *The King of Limbs* become clearer. A conception of nature that is so meaningfully multi-faceted, indeed, alludes to both positive and negative aspects: on the one hand, the image of the earth as a symbol of rebirth, flourishing and therefore life; on the other hand, the idea of a hostile, nonhuman (and, in a sense, also superhuman) dimension, merciless and indifferent to human life, at times untamed and attributable, in certain ways, to the dark, impenetrable space of the human subconscious, where involuntary urges and insurmountable drives lie, undisturbed. This conception of nature is, incidentally, meaningful to the present investigation, as it shares the antinomical and polarizing character that, as we tried to explain, is also typical of technology and represents, depending on the context, a benefit to human beings or, on the contrary, a potential danger.[48]

---

48 From a certain point of view, it is not bold to suggest that *The King of Limbs* is the (technological) glorification of an auditory universe tied to nature, in the same way that previous albums (especially *Kid A* and *Amnesiac*) were the glorification of an auditory universe related to technology. Therefore, in both cases the band's creative impetus was guided by the desire to explore uncharted territories in original, unprecedented ways: in other words, a territory belonging to a sort of natural condition, on the one hand, and a domain characterized by the primacy of an artificial and technological mindset, on the other hand.

Returning to the obscure mood expressed by the album – or, in other words, the way in which the theme of nature not only influences the lyrics, but is also able to shape the sound texture of *The King of Limbs* – we can say that the band's eighth work was characterized by a musical profile largely built upon synthetic rhythms and evocative digital patterns. Precisely due to the complex and enigmatic nature of their structure, these rhythms and patterns metaphorically seem to recall the abstract dimension of a dark forest enveloped by branches, a gloomy place that is characterized by mythological connotations related to magic and ritual. The element of ritual – that, as is well known, according to many philosophical and anthropological perspectives has played, and continues to play, a constitutive role in the origin itself and the meaning of art and aesthetic experience[49] – is in no way foreign to Radiohead's conception of music. Indeed, this element finds legitimacy especially in the musical context of an album like *The King of Limbs*, not only for the fact that the natural condition of the human beings, to which the album is referring, is conceptually close to the primordial sensorial universe and the fabled-mythological imaginary deeply rooted in the human subconscious and archaic folk traditions – rather than a rational techno-scientific view tied to growth and development of an increasingly artificial culture and society. Those elements are also legitimized in *The King of Limbs* because the aforementioned mythological and ritualistic connotations are associated with new genres and musical features tied to technologies that the band meaningfully chose to explore when creating the album. We are referring to, for example, new trends tied to dance music, like dubstep, 2-step and drum & bass, all rooted in a strong conception of dance as a form of experiencing rituality. In the wake of these musical movements – whose main figures include eclectic artists like Burial, Kode9, Skream and Aphex Twin –, as well as in the wake of the manifestation of a still unspoiled, roaring cultural scene oriented towards the emancipation of electronic music from the more traditional and canonical genres of dance music, Radiohead once again reshaped its artistic

---

49　On this topic, see, for instance, the hermeneutical reflections on the central role played by the dimension of ritual in art and aesthetic experience offered by Hans-Georg Gadamer (1986, pp. 3-53).

language. All of this with the aim, more so than ever, to «appeal to the body» through obsessive rhythms and pulses that, at the same time, brush against the rave dimension of this music that «tends towards the mysticism of unconsciousness and a sense of exhilaration realized through dance.[50]»

The album's opening track, «Bloom,» presents multiple, overlapping synthetic rhythms produced by analog instruments that are slightly asynchronous. Their constant repetition imparts the song with a hypnotic quality, transporting the listener to a dimension that is at times dreamlike, like a sort of trance. Towards the middle of the song a melody begins to psychedelically germinate over the constant rhythmic pulsing (created by a guitar played with the bow and simultaneously a synthesizer), remotely evoking the hypnotic, whirling and spinning atmosphere of a song like «Tomorrow Never Knows» by The Beatles. *The King of Limbs* is permeated, as a whole, by a vibrating, constant and fundamental rhythmic component that generates a tension somewhere between nervousness, agitation and excitement, exemplified in its third track, «Little by Little,» a lugubrious, agonizing song, where the groove led by the bass and the guitar, along with the syncopated percussive rhythm that forms the base of the song, outlines the main motif.

In this sense, it is precisely rhythm that probably represents the primordial component of *The King of Limbs* (as well as one the primordial dimensions of music in general, as has been explained by various philosophical-anthropological conceptions of music), not only because it naturally and instinctively inspires bodily movements, but also because it often requires of the listeners, due to its immediacy, less intellectual requirements to be understood, appreciated and enjoyed. From a certain point of view, the concept of rhythm symbolizes here the heartbeat, the archaic and primordial pulse *par excellence* that accompanies all human beings from the prenatal phase within the mother's body and that, because of this, activates a sort of rhythmic imprint in the unconscious memory of each living creature. As difficult as it may seem to understand human nature (as it often is quite elusive and undecipherable), on the base of the aforementioned reasons one can suggest that it

---

50   Alfieri 2019, p. 72.

is essentially tied to a sense of rhythm, in the case of the natural physiological-corporal pulsations within our body, as well as in the case of artificial beats.

A quick mention of the aesthetics of Steve Reich can be meaningful in this context, an outstanding American composer often included in the movement of 20th-century minimal music. As per Reich's musical career, if one wishes to find «an element that is present in almost every one of his works, it would be *pulse*.[51]» As we will see in the next chapter, among the significant experiences Radiohead had in recent years, that contributed to the definition of the band's unique position within the contemporary music scene (in reference to both «light music» and «serious music,» to once again make use of Adorno's terms[52]), we must precisely include certain experiences that put Radiohead into contact with a rigorous avant-garde composer like Reich. For the moment, regarding Reich's original and indeed unmistakable musical aesthetics, and in reference to the aforementioned rhythmic dimension, we will simply add here that

> [n]o matter what piece you listen to from the American composer [...] what strikes the ear is the presence of a sort of «pulsing pattern» that regularly acts as the background of the entire musical discourse, beyond all the potential variations in rhythm, melody, and harmony. Moreover, the relevance of the category of «pulse» was underlined by Reich himself in 1970 and cited as a feature of music of the future [...]. In some way, this aspect can be considered the veritable

---

51   Fronzi 2021, p. 209.
52   Adorno 1976, pp. 21-38. To be precise, the English title of the second chapter of Adorno's *Introduction to the Sociology of Music* is «Popular Music,» rather than «Light Music.» However, as precisely observed by the book translator in his Notes to Adorno's text (p. 229), Adorno himself noted in the Preface to his *Introduction to the Sociology of Music* that many ideas expressed in the second chapter had been «previously laid down in an English essay ("On Popular Music," *Studies in Philosophy and Social Science*, Vol. IX, No. I, p. 17 ff., written, "with the assistance of George Simpson," while Adorno headed the music division of the Princeton Radio Research Project).» So, in translating from German into English Adorno's *Introduction to the Sociology of Music*, the translator chose to use «the terms of that essay,» i.e. «On Popular Music,» although the German title of the second chapter of Adorno's *Introduction to the Sociology of Music* is *Leichte Musik* («Light Music»).

fil rouge that cohesively holds together a musical production that is undoubtedly rich and diversified. [...] Minimalism – from which even so-called «popular music» freely drew from, starting with the psychedelic rock of the 1970s – moves away from the post-Webernian European musical avant-garde: it prioritizes the study of essential structures, developing new temporal dimensions and, most importantly, stimulating original modes of perception.[53]

«Lotus Flower,» perhaps one of the most famous songs from *The King of Limbs*, is built upon a captivating rhythmic motif in which the beat of the drums and clapping hands weave together to create a fertile, alluring sound texture with the notes of the electric bass. The sinuous, meandering soul-funk melody grows out of this background, representing the main motif, embodied by Yorke's languid yet vibrant falsetto: «There's an empty space inside my heart where the weeds take root / So now I set you free, I'll set you free.[54]» The meaning behind the lyrics, which are rich with metaphors and analogies dedicated to a natural realm, seems to allude to the pursuit of a more spontaneous, natural human dimension, in some way free from social conditioning, in which even the relationships between individuals, despite their complexity, can be experienced with an attitude of open sincerity: «Slowly we unfurl as lotus flowers [...] Listen to your heart.[55]» As a final analysis, in reference to the title of the song, «the symbolic meaning of the lotus flower should not escape us, traditionally associated with purity [...] and rebirth.[56]»

«Feral,» the fourth track on *The King of Limbs*, seems to be a mix of sampled digital electronic sounds, arranged around a central rhythmic pulsing. It is undoubtedly the most digital, experimental and technological song on the album, as it is characterized by sounds that are close to ambient music and dubstep, as can be seen in the first bars. It seems to be a frenetic sequence of sounds and synthetic rhythms reproduced by a deranged computer. Even the lyrics, manipulated with digital instruments, are merely vocalized fragments, apparently disconnected and randomly arranged:

---

53 Fronzi 2021, p. 209.
54 Radiohead 2017, p. 266.
55 Radiohead 2017, p. 267.
56 Solventi 2018, p. 262.

«You are not mine. / I'm not yours. / It's all fine. / Please don't judge.[57]» In this regard, it can be interesting to cite here the apt observations included in a review of *The King of Limbs*:

> It's not pop, it's not electronic, it's not rock. Then, what exactly is *The King of Limbs*? It's a halfway point between everything, a mix in which you can find traces of the old Radiohead, although in the context of a game of shadows that makes the album perhaps the most mysterious and difficult to categorize yet. [...] There is little left of the pop beauty from their previous album; here the band is bolder. The sound is more compact and monolithic than ever, without, however, forgoing the occasional variation on a theme. [...] A short record – thirty-seven minutes – but extremely dense, perhaps the most introspective, difficult and solid in the history of the band.[58]

As we have shown regarding the glorification of melodic expressiveness, in reference to the style of the band's compositions (especially on *In Rainbows* and, in general, in what we have defined as the third stage of Radiohead's evolution), the presence of sinuous, singable melodies that are also catchy, so to speak, in an imposingly technological sound texture, has the task of bringing the band's energy back to «a human, psychological and existential dimension,[59]» once again opening the path towards possible technological scenarios whose end, however, is to glorify the poetic language of humans rather than technology itself. If this is the case, then «Separator,» the closing track of *The King of Limbs*, is able to reestablish, in this sense, the centrality of the human dimension in the aesthetic universe of the band. This occurs through the establishment of a harmonic, limpid melody that gradually emerges from the repeating, persistent rhythmic drumming and, above all, through the symbolic conclusion of the band's journey through the digital and technological wilderness influenced by dance atmospheres. Following a sort of natural climax, the vibrant final guitar picks outline a sparkling motif that is poignant in its simplicity, and the thin melodic webs become increasingly vivid presences «overwhelmed by the rich timbres of reverb that

---

57   Radiohead 2017, p. 265.
58   Asquini 2011,
59   Alfieri 2019, p. 72.

dreamily float away»: even the songs' lyrics allude to a sort of re-awakening from an unconscious and illusory condition that is typical of dreams, a «dream [...] that is consumed like a moment of connection with the other part of the self, the part that calls to us from the depths.[60]» Indeed, as Yorke sings: «It's like I've fallen out of bed from a long and vivid dream, / The sweetest flowered fruits were hanging from the trees, [...] / And if you think this is over then you're wrong. [...] / Like I've fallen out of bed from a long and vivid dream. / Finally I'm free of all the weight I've been carrying. / Wake me up, will you wake me up?[61]» Once again it is technology, in new and innovative forms, that constitutes and symbolizes the band's preferred method to interpret a reality that is increasingly fragmented, artificially computerized and virtualized, in order to restore an authentic existential meaning to the human condition. So, the technological dimension that is characteristic of *The King of Limbs* – centered, as we stated earlier, on the search for a rhythmic element influenced by the hypnotic tribalism born of new music genres like dubstep, ambient and drum & bass, innervated by «a feeling of synthesis and research, a research within synthesis[62]» – also becomes the key to accessing deeper, lesser-known inner dimensions.

5.

In 2016 Radiohead released what is still today the band's last studio album, *A Moon Shaped Pool*. Once again in this album, digital sounds and synthetic rhythms prove to be an important component in the aesthetics of the band, but this new record is much less wild («Feral!») compared to the previous one, as it is actually rather an intimate and introspective work. Despite the sophisticated musical constructions and the meticulous digital sounds, *A Moon Shaped Pool* does not present itself – and does not seem to aim to present itself – as an opus that is strictly experimental, for various reasons. Firstly, *A Moon Shaped Pool* is not characterized

---

60 Solventi 2018, p. 265.
61 Radiohead 2017, p. 273.
62 Solventi 2018, p. 271.

by the subversive intention of arriving at a new sound or at a sort of emancipation from the band's previous sound: on the one hand, because in 2016 digital music drawing from dance genres, by now an integral part of the mainstream and pop-rock music scenes, had already begun generating rather elaborate, avant-garde sounds manipulated by softwares; on the other hand, because the fundamental intention of the album seems to be that of giving shape to a hidden, mysterious aesthetics of the landscape of our inner world.

The sound texture of *A Moon Shaped Pool*, even in its complexity, is dominated by a general sensation of formal balance, where a search for a sound through technology is able to perfectly coexist with musical qualities and dimensions that are much more traditional, like in the case of the folk/acoustic sounds with echoes from the 1960s and 1970s that can be heard in «Desert Island Disk» and «The Numbers,» or (and above all) in the case of the symphonic, orchestral music that probably represents the most innovative and peculiar feature of the album. In fact, the songs on *A Moon Shaped Pool* are embellished with refined scores written for strings, arranged by Jonny Greenwood and performed by the London Contemporary Orchestra conducted by Greenwood: the antinomical pair «technology/soul,» in this sense, appears to be reinstated and in perfect equilibrium, thanks to their codes of expression balanced between the «digital/analog» poles, «almost cold, yet able to powerfully flood over the listener, laden with melancholy and gravitas that has few points of comparison in contemporary pop-rock music.[63]»

The opening track of *A Moon Shaped Pool*, «Burn the Witch,» embodies and summarizes in the first bars the eclectic style of the new album, in which Radiohead's innovative and difficult synthesis of pop-rock, orchestral and electronic music is able to find an appropriate and coherent form, and is ultimately accessible to (and able to be enjoyed by) a wide audience. The orchestral arrangement for strings permeates the sound of the entire song and is marked by the unique application of specific instrumental techniques (*col legno* and *pizzicato*) that involve striking and plucking the strings of the instruments that together create a sort of rhythmic pulse similar to one produced by percussion instruments,

---

63	Solventi 2018, p. 290.

metaphorically bringing together the analog sounds produced by string instruments and the digital sounds of electronic beats. Even the videoclip of «Burn the Witch» displays cultural influences from a variety of sources: for example, it mixes the setting of well known British animated series from the 1970s – more specifically, the stop-motion cartoon *Trumpton* – and the plot of a 1973 horror film entitled *The Wicker Man*. In brief, the citizens of the village of Trumpton enthusiastically welcome an outsider, but this initial solidarity between the townsfolk and the outsider soon proves to be a lie, a trap for the unlucky visitor who, at the end of the video, is asked to climb to the top of a large human-shaped structure made of hay, built by the citizens of Trumpton, which is then lit on fire (with the outsider inside) under the satisfied gaze of the towns-folk. The lyrics of «Burn the Witch» allude to the absurd «climate of tension that is felt in daily life, in which «it is increasingly easy to identify an enemy as the scapegoat of our fears.[64]»

The digital and technological aspect, although certainly an energized force of the entire album, nonetheless remains in the background compared to other foundational thematic elements and structural musical components of *A Moon Shaped Pool*. This idea seems to apply first and foremost in the literal sense, as in the album's songs many electronic sounds emerge from the background almost as if they were coming from a distance compared to the primary melodic line, at times appearing like a proper oblique harmony, which is to say melodic sections other than the main melody that are nonetheless in the same key (for example, the initial passages of «Daydreaming»). Secondly, the same idea is also valid metaphorically, due to the fact that the most important aspects of *A Moon Shaped Pool*, even compared to its complex musical structures, is probably represented by the themes approached by Thom Yorke in each of the album's songs. Indeed, the lyrics seem to touch a delicate, introspective world, and seem to orbit around the theme of loss and the painful end of important relationships (it is likely, based on some reconstructions and interpretations, that the relationship in question was that between Yorke and his first wife Rachel Owen, who, after the couple's split in 2015, sadly died a premature death in 2016, the year *A Moon Shaped Pool*

---

64   Rennis 2018, p. 95.

was released).[65] From this point of view, the lyrics of various songs on *A Moon Shaped Pool* take the shape of intimate confessions, personal attempts to accept a reality in which regret, nostalgia, suffering and hope painfully wreak their havoc.

«Daydreaming,» the second song of the album, expresses the painful realization of the impossibility of rewinding the tape of our lives («it's too late, the damage is done, the damage is done[66]»), symbolically evoked by digital sound effects emerging from a melody that is played backwards. As we have mentioned, the technological sounds remain in the background and travel through it, so to speak, but without ever taking over; «between blasts of noise and orchestral progressions that envelop the listener,[67]» in a suspended, undefined, minimal and almost mystic dimension, Yorke's voice intones the most meaningful and poetic lines of the song: «Dreamers, they never learn, they never learn / Beyond the point of no return, of no return.[68]»

In fact, the aspect of memory is probably one of the common threads that weave through the eleven tracks of *A Moon Shaped Pool*, in which sentimental (and at times heatedly emotional) recollections from the «soul» forcefully emerge in contact with the rational, solid and often cold surface of reality. The concept of memory also finds a concrete affirmation in the story of the creation of the album: in fact, a large part of the album's compositions have a rather long, troubled history. For instance, several songs were written many years prior to their release in 2016, having never found a definitive form. Many of them had been abandoned and then rediscovered by Radiohead, while other songs continued to take on new shapes that were however never definitive, with each incarnation and interpretation featuring changes in structure, configuration, arrangement and sometimes also the title. It is known that this slow, at times frustrating, compositional process, articulated by the gradual selection, exclusion and recombination of elements, has characterized the band's approach from the very beginning. It is equally meaningful, in this sense, to observe how

---

65   See Leight 2016.
66   Radiohead 2017, p. 290.
67   Solventi 2018, p. 293.
68   Radiohead 2017, p. 290.

A Moon Shaped Pool includes so many older works, which, like memories resurfacing from the past, still alive, pulsing and often painful, seem to manifest the need to find a meaning and expression, in order to be conceptually understood.

One of these compositions, perhaps the most famous among the fans of Radiohead, is the touching song «True Love Waits,» which poignantly closes *A Moon Shaped Pool*. This song, first written in 1995 and then played in an acoustic version several times during the band's concerts, is a slow ballad that, this time in line with the rest of the album, is arranged on *A Moon Shaped Pool* for the keyboards, a minimal sound that is at the same time rich with electronic echoes. Digital, ghostly sounds and transversal melodies in the background give depth and, at the same time, a sober, refined and intimate complexity to the final version of «True Love Waits.» The lyrics are the cornerstone of the piece, due to their poignant meaning and touching sincerity, breathing life into an authentic, almost heartbreaking love letter: «Just don't leave, don't leave.[69]» From a specifically musical point of view, the piano version of «True Love Waits» on *A Moon Shaped Pool* celebrates the sound of the work through the timbre of the notes that resonate in the air and in the silence, as well as conceptually in the narrator's inner reflections. It is interesting to note how the lucid timbre of a secondary melody can be heard in the background (from another keyboard), almost as if it had rained down from the moon, delicately embellishing, after the first refrain, the main thematic line of the song, which vaguely recalls the evocative timbres of Claude Debussy. Regarding this song, an article published some time after the release of *A Moon Shaped Pool* observed:

> with its short harmonic progression of long, insistent chords, [«True Love Waits»] unexpectedly touches much of what can be intuited about love. Namely, the fact that it is an unconditional surrender. A total abandon. An infinite care. A strength that lies outside of time and that reveals its true appearance above all when it disappears. A season of extreme stupidity and joy. An attic haunted by ghosts.[70]

---

69   Radiohead 2017, p. 309.
70   Zucco 2016.

Another aspect of *A Moon Shaped Pool* that is interesting to highlight here is the notion of the inner, spiritual journey that seems to wind through the lyrics on the album. It is a journey that, despite all of the obstacles that appear, is oriented towards rebirth and the discovery of new opportunities for the individual, in the hope that, after all, «a tendency, a virtual trajectory[71]» can still be found in this life. In this sense, the verses of the fourth song on the album, «Desert Island Disk,» are illustrative: «Now as I go upon my way, so let me go upon my way, / Born of a light, born of a light. / The wind rushing round my open heart, an open ravine. / With my spirit light, totally alive and my spirit light.[72]» The roving atmosphere of the journey is further expressed by Yorke's unmistakable voice a few lines later («Through an open door way / Across the street to another life. / And catching my reflection in a window, switching on a light / One I didn't know, totally alive, totally released[73]»), ultimately revealing at the end of the song the realization the first-person narrator reaches at the end of his path: «Different types of loves, are possible.[74]»

The journey apparently narrated by an album like *A Moon Shaped Pool* is an introspective voyage that seems to unfold within the wrinkles of an interior time, rather than through external space: it does not describe precise locations nor involve real places, rather the subjective sphere through the temporal lens of the past, present and future. In fact, analyzing the lyrics of the songs on *A Moon Shaped Pool*, the past seems to embody a constant presence that returns to create chaos in the present through images, memories and recollections, while the present seems in search of its own legitimacy and the opportunity to be fully experienced, according to the idea and the hope that there can still be «[a] present to grasp and articulate.[75]» From this point of view, the songs on *A Moon Shaped Pool* are imbued with a sort of existential nostalgia for a dimension that is no longer tangible, yet yearned for and experienced as much as one still can – although, in our view, with no traces of the kind of nostalgic «retromania» that, according to

---

71   Fisher 2014, p. 19.
72   Radiohead 2017, p. 294.
73   Radiohead 2017, p. 294.
74   Radiohead 2017, p. 295.
75   Fisher 2014, p. 14.

Simon Reynolds, has deeply affected and conditioned a great part of pop culture of our time, mostly thanks to Radiohead's open-minded attitude towards new technologies and new styles that has protected the band from falling prey to the potential temptation of a mere revival of past sonorities and clichés, thus allowing to define Radiohead as «isolated modernist hero figures within rock.[76]»

At this point, it is not difficult to establish a connection with some ideas of the social and cultural critic Mark Fisher, and especially with the concept of «hauntology» that he borrows from Jacques Derrida's influential book *Specters of Marx*, in order to apply these notions to the sphere of popular culture, especially to pop-rock music. It is not our intention to formulate a detailed reflection on the philosophical concept of «hauntology» here – a concept that has been recovered and revitalized by Fisher, and that certainly, in its vast and complex implications, is quite distant from the themes of the songs of a pop-rock band like Radiohead. Nonetheless, we think it is possible to establish an interpretive connection based on the nature and the particular type of nostalgic sensibility of an album like *A Moon Shaped Pool*. Indeed, this album, as we have seen, is infused with a fascination for a technology perceived as being able to actualize our melancholy. According to Fisher, the concept of «hauntology» (a neologism resulting from the union of two words: «haunt» and «ontology») is apt to describe «a confluence of artists» who «converged on a certain terrain» and shared «not a sound» but rather «a sensibility, an existential orientation»: for example, «an overwhelming melancholy,» a preoccupation with «the way in which technology materialised memory,» and an idea of the present as filled with absences, i.e. a sort of refusal «to fall into the illusion of presence.[77]» Therefore, the compositions that can be attributed to artists belonging to this category, i.e. «the artists that came to be labelled hauntological,» are usually tied to a shared melancholic temperament towards a time that is no longer actual; consequently, they are haunted by spectral presences that belong to the past (the «no longer[78]») or are shaped around a

---

76   Reynolds 2011.
77   Fisher 2014, pp. 17-18.
78   Fisher 2014, p. 18. To be precise, Fisher speaks of «that which is (in actuality is) *no longer*, but which *remains* effective as a virtuality.»

future that, in its essence, has yet to happen (the «not yet[79]»). In this sense, Fisher notes how «the use of crackle, the surface noise made by vinyl» probably represents «the principal sonic signature of hauntology,[80]» as it is the most recognizable and characteristic sound of a technology that openly (and nostalgically) reclaims its origin in a lost past. As Fisher emphatically (and dramatically) observes:

> Crackle makes us aware that we are listening to a time that is out of joint; it won't allow us to fall into the illusion of presence. It reverses the normal order of listening [...]. We aren't only made aware that the sounds we are hearing are recorded, we are also made conscious of the playback systems we use to access the recordings. And hovering behind much sonic hauntology is the difference between analogue and digital: so many hauntological tracks have been about revisiting the physicality of analogue media in the era of digital ether. [...] No doubt a yearning for this older regime of materiality plays a part in the melancholia that saturates hauntological music. [...] In hauntological music there is an implicit acknowledgement that the hopes created by postwar electronica or by the euphoric dance music of the 1990s have evaporated – not only has the future not arrived, it no longer seems possible. Yet at the same time, the music constitutes a refusal to give up on the desire for the future. This refusal gives the melancholia a political dimension, because it amounts to a failure to accommodate to the closed horizons of capitalist realism.[81]

Returning now to our main discourse on Radiohead's music, the soundscape that surrounds the music of a song like «Tinker Tailor Soldier Sailor Rich Man Poor Man Beggar Man Thief» seems emblematic in the overall opus of *A Moon Shaped Pool*. Indeed, chords produced by a distorted keyboard emerge out of the surface of a spectrum of white noise; very low frequencies and repeating noises create the background for the entire song. This atmosphere is similar to the sound of a badly tuned radio or television, not

---

79   Fisher 2014, p. 18. More precisely, Fisher defines here hauntology as referring to «that which (in actuality) has *not yet* happened, but which is *already* effective in the virtual.»
80   Fisher 2014, p. 19.
81   Fisher 2014, p. 19.

unlike the crackle that is characteristic of «hauntological» music. Furthermore, throughout the song, melodic fragments played backwards surface: reverse audio is a recurring formal theme in *A Moon Shaped Pool* and it can be found in many songs, like «Full Stop» or the aforementioned «Daydreaming,» for example, which use the reverse audio effect even in «the finale of the song, with that disconcerting, grotesque and almost feral "half of my life" that is distorted and played backwards.[82]» In a certain sense, these sounds seem to draw from the aforementioned nostalgic attempt to return to the folds and wrinkles of time, simultaneously alerting the listeners of the status of fiction that is assigned to the musical material they are listening to.

«Glass Eyes,» a subdued piano ballad, is also influenced by the glacial and ghostly allure that is typical of «hauntological» aesthetics, starting with the mysterious lyrics that seem to stage the dialogues of a phone call with a person that does not exist, set in a desolate, industrial and alienating location: «Hey, it's me, I just got off the train, / A frightening place / The faces are concrete grey.[83]» Although the recipient of the call seems to be a disembodied presence, unable to interact with reality – symbolized by the «[g]lassy eyed light of day[84]» –, the song's finale reveals the inevitability of a tangible, unequivocal and human reality perceived by the protagonist: «I feel this love to the core,[85]» reiterates Yorke. This is the same humanity that, veiled behind an inaccessible, codified and continually retouched realm, demands legitimacy and recognition in another fundamental song of *A Moon Shaped Pool*, «Identikit,» in which the climax is reached through the invocations of the refrain: «Broken hearts make it rain,[86]» quite similar, on account of the image of rain that falls down on a desolate humanity, to the famous verses of «Paranoid Android» («Rain down, rain down, come on rain down on me

---

82 About «Daydreaming,» Solventi observes: «[the finale] (almost) resolves every doubt surrounding the meaning of what we are listening to: Thom is speaking to Rachel, with whom he shared half of his life and brought two children into the world» (Solventi 2018, p. 193).
83 Radiohead 2017, p. 298.
84 Radiohead 2017, p. 298.
85 Radiohead 2017, p. 299.
86 Radiohead 2017, p. 300.

/ From a great height, from a great height, height[87]»), the song and, so to speak, the symbol of *OK Computer*. As Stefano Solventi highlights, «despite the seemingly algorithmic deceit with which the posthuman world allows itself to be perceived, it is nonetheless caked in human nature.[88]»

Once again there is a connection between the band's legendary 1997 album, *OK Computer*, and the futuristic imaginary of *A Moon Shaped Pool*, especially in «Decks Dark,» as the lyrics similarly represent the science fiction setting described in a song like «Subterranean Homesick Alien,» with its aliens and spaceships. If, indeed, the lyrics of this song from *OK Computer* alluded to extraterrestrial settings to escape to, in order to distance oneself from the human condition in the contemporary age (with lyrics like «Up above aliens hover making home movies for the folks back home,[89]» and «Take me on board their beautiful ship, / Show me the world as I'd love to see it[90]»), a song like «Decks Darks,» from *A Moon Shaped Pool*, seems to depict a similar futuristic scene, but through an apocalyptic lens, surrounded by a much more negative, hostile atmosphere, as can be seen in the following lyrics: «Then into your life, there comes a darkness, / There's a spacecraft blocking out the sky. / And there is nowhere to hide. / You run to the back and you cover your ears, / It's the loudest sound you've ever heard, / And all we trapped rag doll cloth people, / We are helpless to resist / In our darkest hour.[91]» The themes discussed in the two songs are undoubtedly different and in no way identical, but regardless we consider it possible, interesting and appropriate to underline how, for over twenty years later (after the momentous album *OK Computer*, that we discussed at length earlier in the book), the reference to a technological and science fiction universe was never abandoned by Radiohead, quite the contrary: if anything, it was more deeply explored and understood.

In conclusion, let us examine pieces on *A Moon Shaped Pool* like «The Numbers» and «Present Tense,» that, although revealing

---

87   Radiohead 2017, p. 90.
88   Solventi 2018, p. 291.
89   Radiohead 2017, p. 92.
90   Radiohead 2017, p. 93.
91   Radiohead 2017, p. 292.

different deeper meanings, are mainly connected by the element of the temporal dimension.[92] Indeed, the former, with its psychedelic folk sound (that is quite similar, in certain passages, to the acoustic sagas of Led Zeppelin from the 1970s), is an invocation of the effectiveness and the power of a rigorous, individual initiative in the present moment, as it is revealed the essence of performing a task («One day at a time[93]»), while the latter rediscovers a profound inner reflection through a reference to an unambiguous, unassailable but painful present. The lyrics of «The Numbers» exhume the «humanity/technology» dichotomy, highlighting the idea of nature and the important role it represents for human beings, as well as the idea of respect for the environment. The earth and the human beings are primordially and reciprocally connected, given that, as once noted by the Italian songwriter Giovanni Lindo Ferretti, perhaps «[i]n the world we discover only what is inside of us,» yet «we need the world to discover [what is inside of us].[94]» As one of the most important lines of «The Numbers» tells us: «We are of the earth, to her we do return, / The future is inside us, it's not somewhere else[95]» – despite the fact that contemporary society, blinded by the algorithmic enchantment of technologies that are hungry for more prospects of economic profit, is increasingly distanced from it.[96]

Radiohead's song «Present Tense,» as we have already mentioned, appears like an acknowledgement and awareness of (the individual) present moment, musically inspired by bossa nova rhythms with a swirling, hypnotic atmosphere, as if it were suspended in a spiritual, timeless dimension.[97] The song is

---

92 On the relation between music and time in Radiohead (although with a specific focus on *Kid A*, rather than on the band's last albums), see Lin 2018, pp. 43-53.

93 Radiohead 2017, p. 303.

94 Ferretti and Zamboni 1998, p. 139.

95 Radiohead 2017, p. 302.

96 In this regard, other meaningful lines from this song are: «We call upon the people, the people have this power, / The numbers don't decide, the system is a lie, / A river running dry, the wings of butterflies» (Radiohead 2017, p. 303).

97 In the Introduction we included a quick nod to a critical comparison between the different musical trajectories of bands like Radiohead and Pearl Jam (both «survivors» of the 1990s) that have unfolded over the years.

apparently a declaration of love that inspires a partner dance as a remedy against the tense, painful present that the narrating voice has to face, with lyrics like: «This dance, this dance, / Is like a weapon, is like a weapon / Of self defence, of self-defence, / Against the present, against the present, the present tense,[98]» or even «As my world comes crashing down, / I'll be dancing, freaking out. / Deaf, dumb and blind / In you I'm lost, in you I'm lost.[99]» If taking refuge in an inner dimension, characterized by a sort of suspension of time, to counter the weight of reality («I won't get heavy, no don't get heavy, / Keep it light, and keep it moving. / I am doing no harm[100]»), seems to be the only possible solution, then it is all the same to keep dancing, ceaselessly, yet still «deaf, dumb and blind,[101]» losing oneself once again in a temporary love that, in the present, risks becoming vain and wandering off the path that stretches towards the future. The only weapon against the relentless march of time is music, which, thanks to its autonomous codes and rules, and thanks to its elusive poetic language (ultimately enabling it to «utter the unutterable» and «express the inexpressible[102]»), is able define a

---

Although it is evidently a simple coincidence, it nonetheless appears indicative and meaningful in this context that also the richest song in terms of philosophical implications within the vast discography of the Seattle band is precisely entitled «Present Tense,» included in Pearl Jam's most experimental album, *No Code* (1996). For an interpretation of «Present Tense,» *No Code* and, more generally, the entire «philosophy of Pearl Jam,» we allow ourselves to remind again our readers of the essays collected in Marino and Schembari 2021.

98   Radiohead 2017, p. 304.
99   Radiohead 2017, pp. 304-305.
100   Radiohead 2017, p. 304.
101   Radiohead 2017, p. 304.
102   We borrow these fascinating expressions from Adorno's *Negative Dialectics*, where we read that, «to counter Wittgenstein,» the ambitious aim of philosophical thinking must properly consist in «*uttering the unutterable*. The plain contradictoriness of this challenge,» for Adorno, «is that of philosophy itself, which is thereby qualified as dialectics before getting entangled in its individual contradictions. The work of philosophical self-reflection consists in *unraveling that paradox*. Everything else is signification, secondhand construction, pre-philosophical activity» (Adorno 2004, p. 9; emphasis added). With regard to this, in *Negative Dialectics* Adorno also hints at some fundamental affinities between philosophy and music, for example when he observes: «Philosophy serves to bear out an

specific duration and articulation of the moments of life, like a hidden, silent crack among the ripples of time.

experience which Schoenberg noted in traditional musicology: one really learns from it only how a movement begins and ends, nothing about the movement itself and its course. Analogously, instead of reducing philosophy to categories, one would in a sense have to *compose* it first. Its course must be a ceaseless self-renewal, by its own strength as well as in friction with whatever standard it may have. [...] Philosophy is neither a science nor the "cogitative poetry" to which positivists would degrade it in a stupid oxymoron. It is a form transmitted to those which differ from it as well as distinguished from them. Its suspended state is nothing but the *expression of its inexpressibility*. In this respect it is a *true sister of music*» (Adorno 2004, p. 33, 109; emphasis added).

CHAPTER FOUR
THE CROSS-CUTTING POSITION AND
SUI GENERIS STATUS OF RADIOHEAD
IN THE CONTEMPORARY MUSIC SCENE

1.

There are always different ways to tell a story, whether it be the story of a human relationship, of a historical event, of an abstract concept, of an adventure or misadventure of any kind, etc. The history of the arts and, in this particular case, of music, are no exception, which is why one can undoubtedly say that there are various ways in which a musical phenomenon or event can be interpreted and narrated. One of the possible ways to do so – both in general and in relation to the specific subject of this book – consists of focusing on the relationship between what has traditionally been known as «serious music,» on the one hand, and «popular music» or «light music,» on the other, as well as the (constitutive) relationship between music and technology and the various ways in which this relationship was structured and configured over time. In this final chapter of *The Philosophy of Radiohead* we will focus on what, for a series of reasons, seems to be the special, if not unique and *sui generis*, position of the English band within the contemporary music scene, drawing inspiration from the criteria and topics that we have just mentioned in order to relate this story.

Apropos of the complex question concerning the relation between so-called «serious» and «light» music, and the predominant aesthetic approaches to this topic, Theodore Gracyk has critically noted that, «until recently, the interdisciplinary field of aesthetics [...] was either silent about, or hostile to, popular culture», in general, and popular music, in particular, on the basis of the predominant idea that the latter is *always* and *necessarily* «aesthetically impoverished.[1]» For this reason, although the field of popular

---

1   Gracyk 2007, p. 6.

music studies represents a well established academic field today, for Gracyk most investigations in this field have been developed within frameworks that «value music as a social practice» (or better: understand it «*only* [as] social practice»), like sociology or cultural studies, which demand «evaluative neutrality» in approaching this subject, and which «explicitly dismiss the importance of the music's aesthetic dimension.[2]» Also Richard Shusterman, in the context of his pragmatist aesthetics, has diagnosed a typical tendency of aestheticians and cultural theorists to denigrate the popular arts «as mindless, tasteless trash,» without recognizing the fact that popular art, as Shusterman notes, provides us with «too much aesthetic satisfaction to accept its wholesale denunciation as debased, dehumanizing, and aesthetically illegitimate,» not to mention the fact that popular art often «has the power to enrich and refashion our traditional concept of the aesthetic.[3]»

In this context, should one want to find an example in contemporary aesthetics that can be also useful in the specific context of a philosophical inquiry into the music of Radiohead, one could make reference to the book *Strange Tools. Art and Human Nature* written by the enactivist philosopher Alva Noë. In fact, *Strange Tools* also includes a specific chapter on pop music – a concept, the latter, that Noë uses with a very broad meaning, thus understanding «pop» as including «a whole gamut of musical forms: rock, rhythm and blues, soul, hip-hop, top forty, reggae, but, importantly, not jazz, folk, or the music of the Broadway musical.[4]»

---

2   Gracyk 2007, p. 1.
3   Shusterman 2000, pp. 169, 173, 178. Quite significantly for our discourse, Shusterman's favorite example is precisely rock music, which «can be so intensely absorbing and powerful that it is likened to spiritual possession,» and which «suggest[s] a radically revised aesthetic with a joyous return of the somatic dimension which philosophy has long repressed» (Shusterman 2000, pp. 178, 184).
4   Noë 2015, p. 168. Of course, from a rigorous terminological point of view, it is also possible to observe that concepts like «rock» and «pop,» strictly understood, refer to musical forms that are based on different principles and have diverse aesthetic traits (Mecacci 2011, pp. 147-162). Moreover, one can sometimes argue that «rock,» and not «pop,» must be understood as «a universal language» – «rock is both Elvis and Brian Eno,» and «even what does not sound like "rock," in principle, falls within its history» (Maurizi 2018, p. 141) –, thus drawing the conclusion that «rock» should not be included in the concept of «pop» but, on the contrary, certain artists and

Noë starts from the presupposition that «[i]t is an important fact about pop music» that «[it] looks like music, but it isn't,» because one «can engage with it, in a serious way, without engaging with it *as music*,» but rather appreciate it *only* for external factors such as the exhibition, the spectacle, the aura, the fascination of the star system, the charisma and sex appeal of the musicians, and so on.[5] From Noë's critical point of view, indeed, *all* pop-rock music «is just a vehicle for something else», namely a mere «presentation of, or fabrication of, a character.[6]» On this basis, Noë peremptorily claims:

> Indeed, to engage with pop music as music is, almost always, to fail to engage with it at all. [...] People don't crowd into packed arenas to listen [...]. What matters is the event [...]. When you distill the music out of the pop you lose the value. [...] It isn't about the music. It's about something else. [...] [W]hen we love pop music, what we love, really, truly, is not so much the music; rather, we love the one, the star, there in the spotlight. [...] Pop music is exhibition. It is demonstration. [...] It looks like music, but it isn't. [...] Pop music isn't directed to music. The artist himself stands large and demands that you pay attention to *him*. The music is, at most, a way of directing your attention to him; *he* captures your attention and your fascination. His music is like his words. You look through the music to the person, or to an artistic model of the person. It's not the

---

bands commonly defined as «pop» should be included in the history of «rock.» As once observed by Robert Fripp, «[r]ock is the most malleable musical form we have. Within the rock framework you can play jazz, classical, trance music, Urubu drumming. Anything you like can come under the banner of rock. It's a remarkable musical form. [...] One can, under the general banner of rock music, play in fact any kind of music whatsoever» (Fripp, cited in Tamm 1990, pp. 20-21). Anyway, as has been noted by Gracyk, «musical category is a matter of genealogy as much as sound»: «In viewing a large chunk of popular culture as rock, we operate at a relatively abstract level [...]. As such, "rock" operates largely as an ideological abstraction, not as the label of an observable property of the phenomena it unifies. [...] The concept of rock, like that of jazz, is an umbrella for a wide range of musicians and performance styles with some common antecedents and influences» (Gracyk 1996, pp. XI, 5). On the relation between the concepts of popular music and rock music, see also the contributions of Fisher 2011 and Moore 2011.

5   Noë 2015, pp. 168-172.
6   Noë 2015, p. 182.

what of sound but the *what* of action and personality that interests us when we are engaged with pop music. [...] From this standpoint we can appreciate that it is no accident that pop music is the music of fandom and the cult of personality. [...] Pop stars are sex symbols [...]. [P]op music isn't primarily music. [...] Pop music is the art of pure personal style. [...] The songs of the Beatles, the great ones, are fine songs, but their greatness lies elsewhere, in, as I can say now, their social meaning.[7]

From our point of view, it can be said that a philosopher like Noë, in presenting his aesthetic conception of pop-rock music, is right *only to some extent*: that is, it is true that *some* forms of pop-rock music actually correspond to what Noë critically notices about the listeners' interest *only* for the event, the spotlight, the exhibition, the entertainment, the fascination for the pop star's personality and sex appeal etc., instead than being interested in the music *as such*. With regard to the musical material itself, rather than the listeners' preferences, it is also clear that Noë is right *to some extent* when he claims that «[i]n place of rhythm there is only pulse, and in place of voicings there is only [the singer's] cry and the dull pounding of "power" chords»: that is, *some* forms of pop-rock music actually «[do] not invite, and maybe [do] not even repay, close listening». In other words, «musically speaking», it is true that *some* pop-rock music, as Noë claims, «may be simple-minded and unsophisticated, clichéd and predigested», and *some* songs are «conventional» and «musically – harmonically, rhythmically, melodically, structurally – [...] simple.[8]» Anyway, in our view, while these critical ideas are probably true in the case of *some* forms of pop-rock music, *some* artists and *some* songs, they are also untrue in the case of others. In other words, a radically critical perspective like Noë's is only partially true, although Noë, following a certain trend that has been quite typical in the philosophical criticism of popular culture, rather tends to present his views in the form of «totalizing claims[9]» that problematically aim to be equally valid for *all* pop-rock music, from Madonna and Beyoncé to Bob Dylan, Jimi

---

7   Noë 2015, pp. 168, 170-172, 175, 177, 180.
8   Noë 2015, pp. 169, 171.
9   Shusterman 2000, p. 169.

Hendrix, Bruce Springsteen, Lou Reed, Neil Young and David Byrne (limiting ourselves to some of the names effectively quoted by Noë to exemplify his thesis).

At this point, however, it is intriguing to note that Noë himself admits in *Strange Tools* that *some* phenomena in the field of pop-rock music are able to overcome the limits of his own dichotomous scheme, according to which «the classical musician displays the music in his or her performance,» whereas «the pop musician displays himself or herself.[10]» In other words, also Noë admits the existence of *some* phenomena in the field of pop-rock music that *cannot* be adequately grasped if we limit ourselves to such dualistic interpretive patterns. Apropos of this, quite interestingly for the specific discourse developed in the present book, the fitting example used by Noë is precisely that of Radiohead, a pop-rock band that, for him, fascinatingly occupies «a sort of in-between place» or transversal position: «a position in the world of pop while at the same time consistently concealing themselves behind their music, creating music that commands attention and fascination *as* music.[11]» In this final chapter we will attempt to investigate this kind of *sui generis* position in the contemporary music scene that Radiohead has apparently occupied, believing that this will also prove to be important in order to understand some other aspects and implications of what we have called in our book the «philosophy of Radiohead.»

2.

In the previous chapters, in order to present our philosophical interpretation of Radiohead's musical aesthetics, we often turned our attention to the «philosophical musicology[12]» of Theodor W. Adorno. From Adorno's point of view, the question of technology – that, as we have seen, fruitfully acted as a common thread in our attempt at analyzing Radiohead's musical production, both in terms of form and content – is fundamental

---

10 Noë 2015, p. 182.
11 Noë 2015, p. 175.
12 See Rognoni 1966.

at various levels. These levels include, for example, Adorno's critique of contemporary society – in which it is impossible to silently ignore «the false aspects of present-day technocratic praxis[13]» at all levels – as well as, in equal measure, his philosophical examination of art and, more specifically, music. This is confirmed by the centrality of Adorno's dialogue with the illuminating perspectives of his colleague and friend Walter Benjamin on the artistic changes determined by the advent of technological reproducibility (a concept that Benjamin primarily illustrated with the example of film, while Adorno approached the concept through music[14]), and also by the vital importance of the theme of artistic technique in Adorno's wide musicological oeuvre, as well as in his posthumously published *Aesthetic Theory*.[15] For example, in defining his concept of the «inherent tendency of musical material» in *Philosophy of Modern Music*, his musicological masterpiece from 1949, Adorno explains he is referring to «[t]he most progressive level of technical procedures» available in, and suitable to, each phase of development in the history of music, the «correctness or incorrectness» of which (since for Adorno, in music there is not so much what is agreeable or disagreeable, beautiful or ugly, but what he ambitiously considers correct and true or, vice-versa, incorrect and false) is *not* decided by their «isolated appearance,» but rather must be judged and measured «only from the perspective of the level of technique adhered to at a given time.[16]» Consequently, for Adorno,

> the truth or falsity of all musical detail is dependent upon [the] total state of technique, [and] this level will be evident only in the specific configurations of the compositional tasks. No chord is false «in itself,» simply because there is no such thing as a chord in itself and because each chord is a vehicle of the total context – indeed, for the total direction. [...] But at this point the picture of the composer is also transformed. [...]. He is no longer a creator. [...] The state of

---

13   Adorno 1977b, p. 88.

14   On the important correspondence between Adorno and Benjamin, see the rigorous study carried out by Chitussi 2010.

15   On the persisting significance and actuality of Adorno's aesthetic theory today, see the contributions collected in Gandesha, Hartle and Marino 2021.

16   Adorno 2016, pp. 22-23.

technique appears as a problem in every measure which he dares to conceive: with every measure technique as a whole demands of him that he do it justice and that he give the single correct answer permitted by technique at any given moment. The compositions themselves are nothing but such answers – nothing but the solution of technical puzzles.[17]

In *Music and Technique*, a 1958 essay specifically dedicated to further outlining the relationship between the two concepts, Adorno quite lucidly and precisely clarifies:

> The meaning of the Greek word *techne* from which both «technique» and «technology» are derived offers an indication of the unity of this concept with art. If art is the external representation of something internal, the concept of technique embraces everything which pertains to the realization of that interior substance. In the case of music, not only the realization of spiritual substance in notes is involved, but the transformation which makes these notes accessible to sensory perception as well. In short, both production and reproduction are involved. Musical technique embraces the totality of all musical means: the organization of the substance itself and its transformation into a physical phenomenon. [...] By virtue of its technical organization the work of art attains to a context of meaning; everything in the work is able to legitimize itself in terms of technical necessity.[18]

Then, in his reflections on the relationship between music and technique, Adorno goes on to observe that

> [t]he concept of technique encompasses its own dialectic. That the expression «technique of composition» – no matter how old the actual practice itself might be – is of relatively recent coinage offers an indication of this. The term was hardly used at all before the 19th century. It makes its appearance only with the advent of artistic self-reflection within the act of composition, with the consciousness of progressive domination over tonal material by the means of compositional invention, and with the increasing freedom in the disposition of these means which themselves achieve autonomy through

---

17   Adorno 2016, p. 23.
18   Adorno 1977b, pp. 79-80.

this very process. [...] Ever since music came to share emphatically in progress – in industrial progress, that is – ever since the *Symphonie fantastique* of Berlioz, music too, like the entirety of industrial society, has had to pay the price for this progress. Unless appearances lie, this development has today reached an extreme. [...] Technological development, understood at first as extra-musical, then guarded by compositional intentions, converges [today] with inner-musical development. If works of art become their own reproduction, it is then foreseeable that reproductions will become works. With the absolute acoustic realization of a composition through electronic means, indeed, perhaps even by means of recording on wire or tape, doubts are registered regarding the writing down of a manuscript score [...]. Attempts in opposition to this to preserve a refuge removed from technification for portrayal, spirit, or meaning are struck down by impotence.[19]

There are many elements in these quotes from Adorno that are not only interesting in and of themselves, but that are also useful for our attempt to develop a philosophical reflection on Radiohead's music. Indeed, as this excerpt shows, in the 1950s Adorno perfectly understood the evolution (that, for him, was nevertheless not free of elements of regression) that led from a general idea of musical technique to a more specific notion of compositional technique all the way to technology itself – and, in regards to the latter, with a reference to so-called integral serialism and also to the first pioneering experiments of electronic music and *musique concrète* tied respectively to the different orientations adopted at the Cologne laboratory of electronic music, initially led by H. Eimert, and the Paris *Groupe de Recherche de Musique Concrète*, led by P. Schaeffer. What emerges from that excerpt from Adorno's essay *Music and Technique*, beyond the previously discussed notions, is a particularly lucid and clear awareness of the fact that, in the age of the now inescapable technification of music, all of the «[a]ttempts to preserve a refuge removed from technification for portrayal, spirit, or meaning» are ultimately naïf and fatally doomed to failure. Now, if we replace in this quotation the word «spirit» with the word «soul» (that we consciously and ambitiously chose to include in the subtitle of our work), and

---

19   Adorno 1977b, pp. 80, 82-83.

if we take into account what has been discussed in the previous chapters in regards to Radiohead's willingness after *OK Computer* to aggressively technologize the band's aesthetics to find new forms of expression of its «soul» (rather than linger in nostalgic, fruitless attempts at preserving the «spirit» in spaces presumably free from technology): if we take all this into consideration, then it is easy to understand the innovative level of the artistic work completed by Thom Yorke and the other members of Radiohead from the late 1990s until today. Let us also consider that the aforementioned considerations of Adorno from the 1950s were entirely and exclusively focused on the sphere of so-called «serious music» (and, more precisely, on the domain of experimental, radical, avant-garde music), whereas a band like Radiohead belongs to the pop-rock genre, and thus to the general sphere of popular music. Regardless, Radiohead was able to gradually carve out a truly unique space within this latter area.

As we have highlighted in the previous chapters, technology (like other human phenomena), if attentively observed from a dialectical point of view, seems to exhibit positive and fruitful qualities, counterbalanced by negative, adverse ones. «Technology is intrinsically ambiguous: it is a creator of good just as much as a creator of evil,[20]» so to speak: in other words, it seems to constantly unite two contradictory terms or dimensions, almost as if they were two sides of the same token, able to be defined by conceptual pairs like humanization/dehumanization, amelioration/deterioration, liberation/condemnation, empowerment/enfeeblement, safety/danger, success/failure, progress/regression, etc. One of the difficulties posed in conceptually grasping and defining technology, and therefore developing a fixed, unequivocal opinion in its regards, is caused by its ambiguous nature that certainly does not facilitate passing unanimous, equivocal and one-sided judgments. To concisely and immediately exemplify this idea – with a reference to technology viewed from a broad sociocultural perspective, rather than a strictly musical perspective – we can see how technology has undoubtedly supported human beings in their adaptation to the natural *environment* and in the construction of a *world*

---

20   Nacci 2000, p. 51.

that is social and cultural (and thus artificial, in a certain sense),[21] empowering their ability to survive, grow and develop. At the same time, however, technology also seems to expose human beings to a greater number of unforeseen risks that are varied in nature and often unpredictable in terms of their long-term consequences. This produces a dynamic that is simultaneously progressive and regressive, which is difficult to express with unequivocal formulations and unilaterally positive or negative judgments, rather requiring the use of a broad, complex, multifaceted perspective able to express the many nuances of this phenomenon.

To once again make use of examples that are simple, specific, widely familiar and also pertaining to the lyrics of many of Radiohead's songs, it is almost impossible to deny, on the one hand, how the development of technological innovations has led to unheard of and unimaginable improvements in various aspects of contemporary life; on the other hand, however, these same developments and innovations seem to have likewise produced (and still continue to produce) irreversible side effects. The development of virtual communication, mobile phones and instant messaging apps, for example, offers tremendous advantages for the individuals in terms of time, space and the almost infinite possibilities of relationships and interactions they allow, but with the unpleasant consequence of an impoverishment of many relationships, an increased superficiality of our world-experience and our communication with other people, and a paradoxical tendency to produce feelings of isolation in a world in which we are always globally connected. The propagation of an invisible network seems to simultaneously display reassuring and unsettling qualities, transparent yet disorienting, capable to favor

---

21   The distinction between the concept of «environment (*Umwelt*)» – fundamental for understanding the relationship non-human animals have with reality – and the concept of «world (*Welt*)» – as characteristic of the unique relationship that humans have with reality that distinguishes them as rational, linguistic and cultural creatures – is a central distinction within a tradition of contemporary thought that (also in connection with the important notion of «second nature») connects thinkers that otherwise hold quite disparate, distant positions, like Scheler, Gehlen, Heidegger, Gadamer, McDowell, MacIntyre and still others. On this topic, and especially regarding the aesthetic implications and repercussions of these concepts, see Marino 2015 and 2020.

anonymity and heteronomy at a social level, stimulating but also diminishing our attention and ability to concentrate. In brief, «[t]hese changes, in addition to being massive and transformational, were also unexpected and unplanned»: they happened so fast, perhaps too fast, especially at the beginning of the new century, «before we had a chance to step back and ask what we really wanted out of [these] rapid advances.[22]» Many of Radiohead's songs, from the period of *The Bends* to that of *The King of Limbs* and beyond, seem to resolutely and coherently deal with the contradictions of technology, analyzed and expressed at the level of both the form and the content of Radiohead's songs. This allows the band to avoid being imprisoned, enchanted or suffocated by technology, instead transforming it into an instrument worthy for the expression of our «soul» in an age in which it is no longer possible to live without technology.

3.

Returning to Adorno, equally central to his musicological re-flection (and just as crucial in our investigation of the «philosophy of Radiohead» in this final chapter) is the question of the relation-ship between the two spheres of music respectively labeled, as we said, as «serious music» and «light music» (or «popular music»). Although these two spheres *cannot* be reduced into simplified and trivially dualistic categories used to classify contemporary culture and mechanically subdivide it into highbrow or lowbrow, simple or complex, avant-garde or kitsch,[23] high culture or masscult (with a determining role potentially played by midcult as well[24]), it is nonetheless clear that an orthodox Adornian approach tends to understand these two spheres of music as separated by an abyss. In fact, according to Adorno, after Mozart's *Magic Flute* «it was never again possible to force serious and light music together,» and today «[t]he unity of the two spheres of music is thus that

---

22   Newport 2019.
23   Greenberg 1957.
24   Macdonald 1962.

of an unresolved contradiction.[25]» Indeed, as Adorno explains in his seminal 1938 essay *On the Fetish-Character in Music and the Regression of Listening*:

> All «light» and pleasant art has become illusory and mendacious. What makes its appearance aesthetically in the pleasure categories can no longer give pleasure, and the promise of happiness, once the definition of art, can no longer be found except where the mask has been torn from the countenance of false happiness. [...] The new phase of the musical consciousness of the masses is defined by displeasure in pleasure. [...] The diverse spheres of music must be thought of together. Their static separation, [...] the neat parcelling out of music's social field of force is illusionary. Just as the history of serious music since Mozart as a flight from the banal reflects in reverse the outlines of light music, so today, in its key representatives, it gives an account of the ominous experiences which appear even in the unsuspecting innocence of light music. It would be just as easy to go in the other direction and conceal the break between the two spheres, assuming a continuum which permits a progressive education leading safely from commercial jazz and hit songs to cultural commodities. [...] The illusion of a social preference for light music as against serious is based on that passivity of the masses which makes the consumption of light music contradict the objective interest of those who consume it. It is claimed that they actually like light music and listen to the higher type only for reasons of social prestige, when acquaintance with the text of a single hit song suffices to reveal the sole function this object of honest approbation can perform. The unity of the two spheres of music is thus that of an unresolved contradiction. [...] The whole cannot be put together by adding the separated halves, but in both there appear, however distantly, the changes of the whole, which only moves in contradiction. [...] If the two spheres of music are stirred up in the unity of their contradiction, the demarcation line between them varies. The advanced product has renounced consumption. The rest of serious music is delivered over to consumption for the price of its wages. It succumbs to commodity listening. The differences in the reception of official «classical» music and light music no longer have any real significance. [...] The world of that musical life [...] is one of fetishes.[26]

---

25   Adorno 2001, pp. 32, 34.
26   Adorno 2001, pp. 33-35.

Adorno conceived of the two spheres of cultural production – to use a famous expression used in his letter to Benjamin from March 18, 1936 – as «torn halves of an integral freedom, to which however, they do not add up.[27]» This is an idea that, though with a slightly different nuance, is also present in the aforementioned essay on fetishism and musical regression,[28] as well as in the famous chapter on the culture industry in *Dialectic of Enlightenment*, which reads:

> Amusement and all the other elements of the culture industry existed long before the industry itself. Now they have been taken over from above and brought fully up to date. The culture industry can boast of having energetically accomplished and elevated to a principle the often inept transposition of art to the consumption sphere, of having stripped amusement of its obtrusive naiveties and improved the quality of its commodities. The more all-embracing the culture industry has become, the more pitilessly it has forced the outsider into either bankruptcy or a syndicate; at the same time it has become more refined and elevated [...]. Its victory is twofold: what is destroyed as truth outside its sphere can be reproduced indefinitely within it as lies. «Light» art as such, entertainment, is not a form of decadence. Those who deplore it as a betrayal of the ideal of pure expression harbor illusions about society. The purity of bourgeois art, hypostatized as a realm of freedom contrasting to material praxis, was bought from the outset with the exclusion of the lower class; and art keeps faith with the cause of that class, the true universal, precisely by freeing itself from the purposes of the false. Serious art has denied itself to those for whom the hardship and oppression of life make a mockery of seriousness and who must be glad to use the time nor spent at the production line in being simply carried along. Light art has accompanied autonomous art as its shadow. It is the social bad conscience of serious art. The truth which the latter could not apprehend because of its social premises gives the former an appearance of objective justification. The split between them is itself the truth: it expresses at least the negativity of the culture which is the sum of both spheres. The antithesis can be reconciled least of all by absorbing light art into serious or vice versa. That, however, is what the culture industry attempts.[29]

---

27 Adorno and Benjamin 1999, p. 130.
28 Adorno 2001, p. 35.
29 Horkheimer and Adorno 2002, pp. 107-108.

Starting with the meaningful essay *On the Social Situation of Music* (1932), moving then to his fundamental contributions *On Jazz* (1936) and *On Popular Music* (1941), and arriving to *Introduction to the Sociology of Music* (1962), a fundamental belief for Adorno was that *all* popular music of his time, also in virtue of its indissoluble connection with the conditioning power of the culture industry, was *always* marked by standardization and pseudo-individualization. For Adorno, this, alongside the relentless advance of popular music and its (aesthetic and social) untruth, also establishes its fundamental difference from so-called serious music, or more precisely what Adorno emphatically called «good serious music.[30]» For Adorno, in the age in which the «power of the banal» inescapably «extends over the entire society,» the authentic task of art must be identified in the capacity to fulfill a veritable «flight from the banal[31]» and also the capacity to «bring chaos into order[32]» – which, for him, unfortunately *cannot* be applied to «light music» of the 19th and 20th centuries, due to its total collapse (according to Adorno) into the reign of banality, standardization and trivial clichés.

However, starting in the final years of Adorno's life (who died unexpectedly in the summer of 1969, the same summer in which the legendary Woodstock Festival was held), pop-rock music began to manifest signs of experimentation that clearly indicated the possibility to use non-standardized musical materials also in this field. A large part of the most original and nonconformist music from the 1960s, 1970s and 1980s can probably be categorized as such, and this leads directly to the musical landscape of the 1990s and all it has offered, including the band that is at the center of this book: Radiohead. The rapid, continuous and seemingly unstoppable artistic evolution of Thom Yorke and the other members of the band, led by an attempt to establish a driving, dynamic relationship between music, technology and soul, seems to offer a wide catalog of examples that support this claim. This contributed significantly to the confirmation of what we can emphatically define the *sui generis* position of Radiohead in the current music scene.

---

30   Adorno 2009, p. 284.
31   Adorno 2001, p. 34.
32   Adorno 2005, § 143, p. 222.

In speaking about *Pablo Honey* and also, in some ways, *The Bends*, it could still make sense to describe the band's sound as «melancholic pop [...] distinguished by the lead singer's plaintive timbre.[33]» However, already the subsequent album *OK Computer* – rightly defined in an emphatic and ambitious way as «one of the key albums from the last decade of the century[34]» – was obviously characterized by the changes that occurred during the band's transition to «a far-reaching electronic rock, at times even epic and monumental like a post-progressive symphony from space.[35]» Lastly, works like *Kid A* and *Amnesiac* can undeniably be defined as «albums with a decidedly radical sound, that in some ways [recall] the most sophisticated forms of progressive rock.[36]» This, among other things, favors and indeed requires a redefinition of the relationships between the aforementioned spheres of «serious» and «popular» music that, during Adorno's time, were probably more clearly separated than today. In *The Rest is Noise: Listening to the Twentieth Century* (unsurprisingly listing Radiohead's songs among the recent musical phenomena that contributed to reshaping certain views of the music scene), Alex Ross writes:

> Extremes become their opposites in time. Schoenberg's scandal-making chords, totems of the Viennese artist in revolt against bourgeois society, seep into Hollywood thrillers and postwar jazz. The super-compact twelve-tone material of Webern's Piano Variations mutates over a generation or two into La Monte Young's *Second Dream of the High-Tension Line Stepdown Transformer*. Morton Feldman's indeterminate notation leads circuitously to the Beatles' «A Day in the Life.» Steve Reich's gradual process infiltrates chart-topping albums by the bands Talking Heads and U2. There is no escaping the interconnectedness of musical experience [...]. At the beginning of the twenty-first century, the impulse to pit classical music against pop culture no longer makes intellectual or emotional sense. Young composers have grown up with pop music ringing in their ears, and they make use of it or ignore it as the occasion demands. They are seeking the middle ground between the life of the mind and the noise of the street. Likewise, some of the liveli-

---

33   Rausa 2005, p. 452.
34   Bertoncelli 1999, p. 194.
35   Bertoncelli 1999, p. 194.
36   Fabbri 2008, p. 178.

est reactions to twentieth-century and contemporary classical music have come from the pop arena, roughly defined. The microtonal tunings of Sonic Youth, the opulent harmonic designs of Radiohead, the fractured, fast-shifting time signatures of math rock and intelligent dance music, the elegiac orchestral arrangements that underpin songs by Sufjan Stevens and Joanna Newsom: all these carry on the long-running conversation between classical and popular traditions. [...] One possible destination for twenty-first-century music is a final «great fusion»: intelligent pop artists and extroverted composers speaking more or less the same language.[37]

4.

It the context of the specific discourse developed in this book, what stands out quite clearly from these reflections is that, from the 1960s onwards, a new tendency to the interpenetration, mutual contamination and mix of different musical genres, forms, contents and levels has emerged. This has multiple ramifications and implications, also for the discourse presented in a book on Radiohead. In approaching the complex and fascinating stylistic evolution of Radiohead in the previous chapters, besides the essential aspect of the transformation in the band's relationship to technology from *The Bends* to *Kid A* all the way to *A Moon Shaped Pool*, we also mentioned the no less interesting influence that certain artists *outside* of the pop-rock scene had on Radiohead. In his research monograph on *OK Computer* Tim Footman has observed that «Radiohead have acknowledged their debt of inspiration to modern classical composers such as Messiaen and Penderecki,» and that in certain ways it was «inevitable that serious classical musicians would wish to return the compliment.[38]» Although the examples used by Footman in the passage included here do not (yet) consider the relationship between the English band and the American composer Steve Reich, it is precisely this relatively recent example that we will now turn our attention to, as it is a particularly relevant one.

---

37   Ross 2007, pp. 589-590.
38   Footman 2007, pp. 193-194.

It is quite evident that Radiohead must be considered an important, let alone indispensable, band for anyone wishing to simply form an opinion on the development of pop-rock music in the last decades. Equally undeniable is that the music composed by Steve Reich must be considered an important, let alone indispensable, phenomenon for anyone wishing to meaningfully understand the adventures of avant-garde music from the late 1960s until today. It is thus intriguing to note how some years ago the musical trajectories of Radiohead (and more specifically, Jonny Greenwood) and Steve Reich intertwined and stimulated each other in a remarkable way. This crossover or intersection ultimately flowed into a composition from Reich with the meaningful title of *Radio Rewrite* (2012), based on the creative reinterpretation of passages and fragments from the songs «Everything in Its Right Place» and «Jigsaw Falling Into Place» (included in *Kid A* and *In Rainbows*, respectively).

In short, the story goes that Reich attended Greenwood's 2011 performance (with the Ensemble Modern) of his own composition, *Electric Counterpoint*, at the Sacrum Profanum music festival in Krakow. Reich was pleasantly impressed by Greenwood's performance and had the pleasure of meeting him after the concert, and so he eagerly listened to the soundtrack Greenwood developed for Paul Thomas Anderson's film *There Will Be Blood* as well as some of Radiohead's songs. Reich was particularly struck by «Everything in Its Right Place and «Jigsaw Falling Into Place» due to their being «very simple and very complex at the same time,[39]» their «very beautiful [...] melodic stuff,[40]» and also their «elaborate harmonic movement. [...] "Well, *it's* three-chord rock *but it's not*, it's very unusual," says Reich.[41]» This interest in the band grew, ultimately leading Reich to decide to use those two fundamental tracks as musical material for a new composition, the aforementioned *Radio Rewrite*. It is important, in our view, to *not* misconstrue this «use» as a sort of appropriation, manipulation, exploitation or veneering through an orchestral rearrangement, rather as an authentic tribute to a musical material that is *itself* rich, original and

---

39 Miller 2013.
40 Pattison 2012.
41 Petridis 2013 (emphasis added).

noble, and *as such* able to be further processed, reinterpreted and developed to derive new, innovative musical combinations. As can be read on the web page dedicated to *Radio Rewrite* on the website of the record label Nonesuch (which released the album in 2012), Reich himself described this intriguing musical project:

> «Over the years composers have used pre-existing music (folk or classical) as material for new pieces of their own. *Radio Rewrite*, along with *Proverb* (Perotin) and *Finishing the Hat – Two Pianos* (Sondheim), is my modest contribution to this genre.» He continues, «Now, in the early 21st century, we live in an age of remixes where musicians take audio samples of other music and remix them into audio of their own. Being a composer who works with musical notation I chose to reference two songs from the rock group Radiohead for an ensemble of musicians playing non-rock instruments: "Everything in Its Right Place" and "Jigsaw Falling into Place".» Reich and Greenwood met in Krakow in 2010 during a festival of Reich's music, where Greenwood gave a performance of *Electric Counterpoint* that its composer liked very much (Greenwood has since performed it many more times, including during a London tribute to Nonesuch's 50th anniversary at the Barbican Centre). Reich says, «When I returned home I made it a point to go online and listen to Radiohead's music and the two songs mentioned above stuck in my head. It was not my intention to make anything like "variations" on these songs, but rather to draw on their harmonies and sometimes melodic fragments and work them into my own piece. As to actually hearing the original songs, the truth is – sometimes you hear them and sometimes you don't.[42]»

On the one hand, it is clear how normalized and ordinary the fusions between «serious» and «popular» music, and sometimes the direct collaborations between avant-garde composers and pop-rock musicians, have become in recent decades. There are numerous examples that we could mention here, but we will limit ourselves to just a few, like the refined arrangement of Lennon and McCartney's songs completed by Luciano Berio in *Beatles Songs* (1965-67), the intriguing reworking and revisiting of David Bowie's work by Philip Glass («*Heroes*» *Symphony*, 1996), the sophisticated

---

42   Reich 2013.

use of a symphonic orchestra in Peter Gabriel's *Scratch My Back* (2010), the innovative and influential experimentations of musicians belonging to *both* the rock and avant-garde genres like Laurie Anderson, Brian Eno, Robert Fripp, Robert Wyatt and Frank Zappa, or the unique (although not musically successful, in our opinion) collaboration between Lou Reed and Metallica for the 2011 album *Lulu*, inspired by the homonymous opera from 1937 by Alban Berg (although the complete, three-act version was not performed until 1979). On the other hand, although it does not stand out as a unique example, in light of the variety of analogous examples we have just mentioned, the relationship between Radiohead and Steve Reich nonetheless stands out for the originality of its outcome, the vivacity of the reciprocal exchange and dynamism between two so apparently different artists, and also its value as a further example of how a band like Radiohead has been able to push itself beyond what seemed to be its limits, starting with a deep, conscious reworking of its relationship with musical technique and technology in general, and gradually experimenting with melody, harmony, rhythm and timbre in ways that allowed the band to carve out a significant space in the current music scene.

It is likely not a coincidence that the two songs that fascinated Steve Reich to the point that he deeply dialogued with them on the compositional level, «Everything in Its Right Place» and «Jigsaw Falling Into Place,» belong to the post-*OK Computer* phase of Radiohead's musical evolution, the phase in which the members of the band, through a serious effort of technical and formal revolution, were able to precisely «become what they are» – to make use of a well known Nietzschean expression.[43] According to Tim Footman, «[t]he sort of response that [Radiohead's] music has received in the classical community gives some indication of how the band is generally perceived»: in fact, «[m]ainstream artists, such as Queen or Phil Collins, get the big, orchestral treatment,» whereas «more credible, niche-oriented acts attract more credible, edgier classical interpreters and collaborators[44]» – and this

---

43 The implied citation is taken from the subtitle of Nietzsche's book *Ecce Homo*, which notoriously reads *How To Become What You Are* (see Nietzsche 2007).
44 Footman 2007, p. 194.

is precisely what happened with Steve Reich's sophisticated and creative treatment of Radiohead's melodies and harmonies in an original composition like *Radio Rewrite*.

5.

Precisely what we can freely call the metamorphoses of «Jigsaw Falling Into Place» facilitate the continuation and development of the argument presented in this final chapter. This chapter started with the traditional, though not unproblematic, distinction between «serious» and «light» music, to then focus on the constitutive and essential relationship between music and technology. On this basis, we also approached the complex and fascinating phenomenon of the relationships and exchanges that can occur today between pop-rock musicians like Radiohead and avant-garde composers like Steve Reich. Now, if there is a form of expression that has marked the 20th-century musical landscape in a particularly penetrating and irreversible way, it is likely jazz, with its articulated history, endowed with specificity and even singularity, marked by so many turning points (even in periods of just a few decades, or sometimes just a few years) that any interpretation aimed at immediately and one-sidedly defining jazz once and for all may appear suspect in principle.

Understanding the aesthetics of jazz is indeed a challenging, complicated task, much more than it may seem at first glance, as it is a musical phenomenon that, because of some of its intrinsic characteristics (such as the primacy of improvisation), as well as its constant mutations and evolutions, has often disrupted all established, consolidated categories that are often used to define music. For example, in her influential essay on the philosophy of music *The Imaginary Museum of Musical Works*, Lydia Goehr aptly noted that «[j]azz is an obvious example» of how «[s]ome kinds of music are regulated by ideals that conflict with the *Werktreue* ideal[45]»: namely, the typical Western ideal from the 19th and 20th centuries of absolute faithfulness to the original work and, in particular, to the original score, in order to offer an exact

---

45   Goehr 1992, p. 255.

interpretation and faithful execution of a piece. In fact, «[w]hereas in classical music performances we strive towards maximal compliance with a fully specifying score,» in other musical genres, like «jazz improvisations» for example, «very different notions of compliance operate»: jazz musicians typically «seek the limits of minimal compliance to tunes or themes,» and in the case of jazz «extemporization is the norm.[46]» We must also emphasize the strong relation between jazz and the aesthetics of «the performative[47]» and «the improvised/the unexpected,[48]» and how on the philosophical level this certainly poses some important questions on the possibility or not to apply certain schemes used to catalog and interpret music, including famous dichotomous distinctions like that of «serious music/light music.»

Now, our aforementioned reference to what we freely called the metamorphoses of «Jigsaw Falling Into Place» was primarily meant to refer to the eminent composer Steve Reich's arrangement of some of Radiohead's songs. However, that expression can be also a reference to the magnificent version of «Jigsaw Falling Into Place» performed by the pianist Brad Mehldau. A sophisticated protagonist of today's jazz scene, both as a soloist and part of a renowned trio, Mehldau is also a musician with a solid classical and academic background (evidenced by his interpretations on the 2017 and 2023 albums *After Bach* and *Après Fauré*, for example), and even an artist plastically open to some electronic experimentations, as testified by his exciting work in duo with drummer Mark Guiliana.

As is well known, large part of modern jazz is based on the use of a wide catalog of compositions known as «standards,» songs considered part of the established jazz canon that are continually reinterpreted and, actually, reworked during performances that involve *a priori* a certain margin (of varying degrees) for

---

46   Goehr 1992, p. 99.
47   In regards to this concept, see especially Fischer-Lichte 2008. However, in mentioning the emergence of a new «performative turn» in 20th-century music, Fischer-Lichte references avant-garde composers like Cage, Stockhausen, Schnebel and Kagel, or chronologically subsequent musician-performers like Laurie Anderson and Diamanda Galas, but never seems to make explicit reference to jazz.
48   See Bertinetto 2022, in particular pp. 19-55, 119-157.

improvisation. In making use of these so-called standards in a particularly intriguing way, modern jazz has attempted to evade being «swallowed» by standardization (despite the fact that Adorno, still in the 1950s, would say jazz had suffered precisely this fate[49]) by employing various creative resources in a skillful, extensive and pronounced manner, the most notable being improvisation and creative interplay between musicians during performances. From this point of view, jazz musicians' adoption of a single song as a starting material from which to develop their own creativity, in ways that have since become more or less typical and recognizable aspects of jazz, is not in itself something entirely new. However, up until relatively recently, although collaborations between jazz and pop-rock musicians were not entirely unheard of (albeit often in the simple and banal form of featuring a jazz virtuoso as a session musician on pop-rock songs), it was still rather rare for the repertory of standards to consistently accept explicitly pop-rock tunes with conviction, also due to the (often undeserved and misleading) stigma of triviality and marketability that a large part of pop-rock music has been subjected to. But recently, these scenes have also undergone a (welcomed) evolution and as such, to mention just a single example, a deservedly famous album from 1996 from the legendary jazz pianist Herbie Hancock (accompanied by a true «super-group» including Michael Brecker on saxophone, John Scofield on guitar, Dave Holland on bass, Jack DeJohnette on drums, and Don Alias on percussion), with the meaningfully explicit title *The New Standard*, proposed certain songs from The

---

49   For Adorno, indeed, in the case of jazz music «[t]he aesthetic act is made into a sport by means of a system of tricks. To master it is also to demonstrate one's practicality. The achievement of the jazz musician and expert adds up to a sequence of successfully surmounted tests. But expression, the true bearer of aesthetic protest, is overtaken by the might against which it protests. [...] If the aesthetic realm originally emerged as an autonomous sphere from the magic taboo which distinguished the sacred from the everyday, seeking to keep the former pure, the profane now takes its revenge on the descendant of magic, on art. Art is permitted to survive only if it renounces the right to be different, and integrates itself into the omnipotent realm of the profane which finally took over the taboo. Nothing may exist which is not like the world as it is. Jazz is the false liquidation of art – instead of utopia becoming reality it disappears from the picture» (Adorno 1997, p. 131).

Beatles, Peter Gabriel, Donald Fagen, Prince and even Nirvana, as new inductions into the realm of jazz standards.

In an analogous manner, but with a somewhat more systematic effort, in almost all of his records Brad Mehldau has also reinterpreted pop-rock songs through an original, sophisticated and never banal jazz lens. Quite relevant to the final chapter of this book is the fact that precisely Radiohead is likely the most intriguing pop-rock group for a cultured, sophisticated and receptive jazz musician like Mehldau, as can be seen in the attention he paid to Radiohead's music while developing his magnificent version of «Jigsaw Falling Into Place,» included in his 4 CD box set *10 Years Solo Live* (2015). Many of Mehldau's albums and concerts include a reworking of one or more of Radiohead's songs: for example, his versions of «Exit Music (For a Film)» on *Songs: The Art of the Trio Volume Three* (1998), *Art of the Trio 4: Back at the Vanguard* (1999) and *Live in Marciac* (2011), «Paranoid Android» on *Largo* (2002) and *Live in Tokyo* (2004), «Everything in Its Right Place» on *Anything Goes* (2002), or «Knives Out» on *Day Is Done* (2005) and *10 Years Solo Live* (2015). To this list of songs reinterpreted by Mehldau, in both live and studio recordings (and both as a soloist and alongside the other members of his jazz trio), we must also add «Little by Little,» a majestic composition from Radiohead's *The King of Limbs* that has often been performed by Mehldau in a delicate, intense version for piano during his concerts. In this regard, it has been meaningfully suggested that:

> If proof were needed of the vitality and relevance of jazz, then Mehldau is it. Using Nick Drake and Radiohead material in his sets as often as Thelonious Monk, [he] has a cross-generational following that includes the kind of fervent young fans more often found pursuing Robbie Williams. [...] [A]s the 1990s waned, hanging out at a Los Angeles club called Largo, he was exposed to «people like Elliott Smith, Fiona Apple, Rufus Wainwright. The first time I heard Nick Drake was someone covering *River Man*. I thought, what the hell was that beautiful evocative thing in 5/4? The chords reminded me of something modal that I had identified with Coltrane, but it was being sung on a guitar. Then people there tipped me on to Radiohead. I was a little burnt out at that time from going out and buying every jazz record that came out.» [...] «Improvisation,» he says, «is one of the big things I use in my own definition of jazz. You have

the ability to make a pretty intricate narrative, to play around with time itself, like a novel does, and your memory, and your expectation of what's taking place. Monk is doing that, Wayne Shorter, Coltrane. Most of my jazz heroes have that narrative aspect. Improvisation usually implies something very non-intellectual at its core, because when it's really working it has a real flow, it's in the moment. But if I listen to Coltrane, he's in the white heat of the moment, but there's also intricacy and complexity; you can enjoy it as a piece of art the same way you enjoy the compositional rigor of a Beethoven symphony or a Bach fugue. And then [you remember] it's being improvised. I think that's what appealed to me as a kid.[50]»

Just like with Steve Reich's use of Radiohead's songs as a primary source of inspiration for *Radio Rewrite*, it is necessary and essential to highlight that, in our view, Mehldau's interpretations must *not* be considered as a mere attempt by a cultured, refined and sophisticated musician to heighten or dignify a simple, banal material from pop-rock music. Indeed, from our perspective, such a reading of this phenomenon would be a glaring mistake and a rather banal misunderstanding of this fascinating musical enterprise. Rather, it is the originality, the elegant musical nature and especially the unique emotional quality of Radiohead's songs in and of themselves that strongly and prominently emerges in a new way from Mehldau's interpretations. Precisely due to their inherent quality, on par with the most canonical and established jazz standards, these songs lend themselves particularly well to being a source of inspiration for Mehldau's imagination and creative improvisation. From this point of view, Mehldau's own words about Radiohead in the booklet of his aforementioned 4 CD box set *10 Years Solo Live* are certainly clear and meaningful. In fact, as Mehldau observes (with a particular focus on «the angst of Radiohead's *Jigsaw Falling Into Place*,» but not limited only to this song):

Radiohead's original version of *Jigsaw*, with Thom Yorke's lyrics and singing, has a feeling in it that is unique to that band – it's like they invented a feeling for their listeners. The feeling is ecstasy, yes, but there is some kind of fear in it, something unsettled, and that

---

50   Mehldau 2005.

yoking of opposites is why this band is so special for me. One hand is grasping at heaven and touching it a bit; much of the body though remains in the world, which is cold and scary. At some point, we don't know where heaven begins and cold and scary ends; they get all mixed up together. When that happens in Radiohead's music, it feels like time stops for a moment. It's a sweet ambivalence.[51]

6.

This ultimately leads to our final, rather delicate topic: what we may symbolically call the «survival» of pop-rock musicians (in terms of their integrity and ability to defend and preserve their artistic dignity) in an age in which, at least to some extent, «surviving» (in a metaphorical sense of this term, related to the residual opportunities to create truly meaningful works of art) has become difficult, almost impossible. This, too, as we will attempt to show, is an extremely relevant aspect of the interpretation we aim to advance in *The Philosophy of Radiohead*. In order to develop a final result from the exploration of the transversal, *sui generis* position of Radiohead within the contemporary music scene, we can once again draw from some important categories and ideas proposed by Mark Fisher in his critique of modern society. Fisher's social and cultural critique, indeed, adopts a specific perspective on the current possibilities and, at the same time, limits of popular culture. This statement is primarily in reference to Fisher's *Capitalist Realism*, a text that has become now quite famous and much discussed «on that ambiguous planet that is known as *cultural theory* in the English-speaking world,» and also in the galaxy of «musicians, artists, writers, and readers of works on cinema and aficionados of that enigmatic phenomenon we often call "pop culture"»: therefore, it is a brilliant example of what we may define a *Kulturkritik* applied to popular culture, «able to meld analyses of consumerist culture and theoretical-political reflections, knowledge of underground discourses and criticism that would have once been labeled as "militant".[52]»

---

51   Mehldau 2015.
52   Mattioli 2018, pp. 8, 12.

In the context of the analysis carried out in this chapter, the incipit of Fisher's book is particularly striking, with its invocation of «one of the key scenes in Alfonso Cuarón's 2006 film *Children of Men*,» in which the protagonist visits a friend who, in a dystopian-apocalyptic world in which no children have been born for decades because of a disaster that has caused mass sterility, avidly yet senselessly dedicates himself to collecting «[c]ultural treasures – Michelangelo's *David*, Picasso's *Guernica*, Pink Floyd's inflatable pig – [all] preserved in a building that is itself a refurbished heritage artifact.[53]» If read from the perspective of a more orthodox *Kulturkritik* (like Adorno's, for example[54]), the incipit of *Capitalist Realism* could provoke a (somewhat positive) sensation of glaring contrasts, in the sense that Fisher compares without distinction (using the label «cultural treasures») one of the artworks that thinkers like Horkheimer and Adorno considered able to critically confront the questions of our age, i.e. Picasso's *Guernica*, and a legendary symbol of pop culture, i.e. the so-called *Pink Floyd Pig*, the helium-filled, pig-shaped balloon ideated by Roger Waters that appeared on the cover of Pink Floyd's 1977 album *Animals* and was subsequently used by Pink Floyd during its concerts, having it fly over the heads of the fans. In other words, Fisher's contemporary *Kulturkritik* spontaneously and freely associates what many cultural critics and social theorists from just forty or fifty years prior considered to be neatly and rigorously separate: the culture industry and popular culture (in this case, Pink Floyd's music) and its adversary, avant-garde art (in this case, Picasso's *Guernica*).[55]

Fisher's discourse, anyway, seems entirely understandable and, above all, completely legitimate in light of the structure our culture has developed in recent decades. What Fisher seems to grasp is that certain products which could surely be defined, according

---

53   Fisher 2009, p. 1.
54   See Adorno 1997, pp. 17-33.
55   Indeed, Horkheimer and Adorno define the culture industry as the «adversary [of] avant-garde art,» inasmuch as the latter «serve[s] truth,» unlike cinema, radio, popular music or magazines that merely represent for them «the aesthetic equivalent of power» (Horkheimer and Adorno 2002, pp. 101, 103) – although after the misadventures of dodecaphony and serial music in the 1950s/1960s Adorno was also perplexed about the avant-garde's capacity to preserve the truth content of art.

to Adorno, as «commodit[ies] in the strict sense,[56]» produced
and commercialized in order to strengthen the already existing
order of «a society of commodities,[57]» are nonetheless capable of
a «flight from the banal[58]» which, for Frankfurt critical theorists,
represents no less than the secret law of development of the history of modern art. This means that, on the one hand, it is undoubtedly appropriate to recognize and reiterate the decidedly industrial and even commodified nature of pop culture products (as
pioneers like Horkheimer, Adorno and other authors had already
noted in the 1930s and 1940s); on the other hand, however, it is
equally necessary to highlight how recognizing this aspect *does
not* necessarily and automatically equate to monolithically catego-
rizing *all* of these products as standardized, preformed and even
predigested. In fact, sometimes (though certainly not always) the
«industrial work of art reaffirms itself as a "commodity" when it
undermines the concept of "commodity" itself»; in other words,
the work of art transcends the commodity form and «disparate,
volatile situations have indeed been witnessed in the realm of the
culture industry.[59]»

In *Capitalist Realism*, Fisher primarily uses the 1990s grunge band
Nirvana, a band that was more or less contemporary to Radiohead,
as an example to touch upon the possibility of pop-rock musicians
that, despite using musical materials that can be defined (according to Adorno) as standardized, are nonetheless able to use them
in non-standardized ways, which is to say a use of these materials
that is free, creative, original, experimental and often critical, or
rich with critical echoes and implications strictly related to both
the aesthetic and the socio-political levels. As Valerio Mattioli underlines in his preface to the Italian edition of *Capitalist Realism*,
for Fisher it was mainly the «danceable avant-garde quality» of

---

56   Adorno 2002b, p. 473.
57   Adorno 2009, p. 135.
58   Adorno 2001, p. 34. On the same question, see also Adorno's letter to
     Benjamin from August 2, 1935, where Adorno writes to his colleague and
     friend: «your conception of the history of painting in the nineteenth cen-
     tury as a flight from photography (to which the flight of music from "ba-
     nality" is an exact correspondence) is powerful» (Adorno and Benjamin
     1999, p. 110).
59   Vitta 2012, pp. 119, 163.

certain music from the 1990s – which «transformed English underground dance music into a never before seen mix of machinic/posthuman desire, especially in the sounds of jungle music and drum & bass music» – that represented the «epitome of [an] irrevocable and in some ways tyrannical future shock,» the path of «a future able to operate in the present, to the point that it can even change it.[60]» This example is particularly interesting in the context of this book since, as we have shown, an important influence for Thom Yorke and his bandmates at the time of Radiohead's electronic-technological turn with *Kid A* and *Amnesiac* was precisely represented by their interactions with several decidedly experimental dance music phenomena.

However, after observing that it is important «to remember the role that commodification played in the production of culture throughout the twentieth century,» and after citing the «dreadful lassitude,» the «objectless rage,» the «wearied voice [of] despondency» and the «high existential angst of Nirvana and Cobain[61]» as a true «sign o' the times» (freely citing here the title of a famous song by Prince), Fisher seems to resignedly cede to a seemingly Adornian prophecy of «the aging of the new music.[62]» At this point, in fact, Fisher indulges in bitter, forlorn considerations on what he critically defines the *«precorporation»* of «materials that previously seemed to possess subversive potentials» and that, according to Fisher's perspective, at a certain point of history *completely* fell into the «pre-emptive formatting and shaping of desires, aspirations and hopes» carried out by the culture industry and the commodification of these materials by means of «capitalist culture.[63]» Fisher, then, goes on to pessimistically identify the consequences of this situation, namely the fact that after Nirvana (a band that, in this sense, seems to take on the appearance of the terminal figure in the history of music, almost as if in a post-Hegelian atmosphere depicting the «end of art» or «death of art[64]») there would *no longer* be any possibility to experience «something *outside* mainstream culture,» since alternative and

---

60   Mattioli 2018, p. 11.
61   Fisher 2009, p. 9.
62   Adorno 1988.
63   Fisher 2009, p. 9.
64   On this topic, see Valagussa 2013; Vercellone 2013; Marino 2022.

independent musical spaces have now become well established «cultural zones [and] dominant styles *within* the mainstream»: according to Fisher, Nirvana was succeeded by «a pastiche-rock which reproduced the forms of the past without anxiety» and by the rise of «hip hop, whose global success has presupposed just the kind of precorporation by capital which [he] alluded to before.[65]»

These considerations are understandable from a psychological and sociological point of view, based on the delusions experienced by Fisher's generation in the second half of the 1990s and the first years of the new century, as well as in aesthetic terms. In general, these reflections are surely useful to develop a critical analysis of the contemporary age. However, we are once again faced with the same risk of generalization and expression of «totalizing claims» that can be found in the critical judgments expressed by the main cultural critics of the 20th century who often leaned towards a conception of modern culture as *entirely* standardized, predigested, predetermined, etc. Contrarily to this point of view, we believe that a counter to the theoretical outcomes of a *Kulturkritik* of this kind is an idea expressed by Adorno in some letters to his colleague and friend Benjamin during their lengthy, intense correspondence,[66] but that he did *not* seem open to considering in his own analyses of popular music: the idea of «*more* dialectics,[67]» i.e. to have a constantly fluid and dialectical point of view, to never fall prey to a static, deterministic and undialectical view of cultural phenomena (including those of mass culture and popular music), to never lose sight of the «internal dialectic tension» of such phenomena, even those that are apparently peripheral or condemned to superficiality, to banality and *post-histoire*,» like pop-rock music «between the 1990s and the turn of the millennium.[68]» After all, as Horkheimer warned at the end of his 1959 essay *Philosophie als*

---

65   Fisher 2009, pp. 9-10.

66   On this specific topic, see Adorno's letters to Benjamin from August 2, 1935 and November 10, 1938 – where Adorno, after having read some new and still unpublished works of Benjamin, criticizes his colleague and friend because of «a certain loss [...] of dialectical consistency» in some of his theories and, expressing himself «in as a simple and Hegelian manner as possible,» explicitly claims that «[Benjamin's] dialectics is lacking in one thing: mediation» (Adorno and Benjamin 1999, pp. 106, 282).

67   Adorno and Benjamin 1999, p. 131.

68   Alfieri 2019, p. 7.

Kulturkritik: «[r]esignation is impossible, as long as a remnant of freedom remains.[69]» More than sixty years later, this warning from the founder of critical theory maintains its enduring relevance and can meaningfully spur thinkers, even in the field of critical studies of popular culture, to *never* stop searching for phenomena that manifest remnants of freedom, originality and non-standardization.

Returning to Radiohead, and finally closing our discourse, this is of great relevance also for a philosophical understanding of this band's musical oeuvre. Indeed, «the decisive importance that Thom Yorke's band had and still has in the global rock scene of recent decades has become an undeniable point of reference,[70]» and at least a part of this «decisive importance» lies in Radiohead's determination, consistency and originality in facing the challenges of the post-Cobain cultural scene as described by Fisher. To truly impress this concept upon our readers, we simply need to refer back to Fisher's description of Kurt Cobain, and his aforementioned «dreadful lassitude,» «objectless rage,» «wearied voice» and «existential angst,[71]» and note how these features are as applicable to Nirvana's songs from 1991 to 1993 (like «Smells Like Teen Spirit,» «Breed,» «Something in the Way,» «Serve The Servants,» «Rape Me,» «Pennyroyal Tea,» etc.), as they are to a Radiohead song like «Creep,» the English band's first hit from their first album, *Pablo Honey* (1993).[72] The main «heroes» of the music scene of the early 1990s almost all saw tragic deaths, at times decades later but dramatic nonetheless: Kurt Cobain (1967-1994) from Nirvana, Layne Staley (1967-2002) from Alice in Chains, Scott Weiland (1967-2015) from Stone Temple Pilots, Chris Cornell (1964-2017) from Soundgarden, Mark Lanegan (1964-2022) from Screaming Trees, and still others. It seems reasonable to suggest that bands like Pearl Jam and Radiohead represent «long-lived bands that saw multiple decades and challenged the abyss of self-destruction which caused

---

69   Horkheimer 1985, p. 103.
70   Alfieri 2019, p. 8.
71   Fisher 2009, p. 9.
72   As we have already mentioned in this book, in 2021 Thom Yorke presented a new, particularly eerie, painful and musically disorienting version of «Creep.»

them to approach today *in different ways.*[73]» The fundamental and distinctive point of this discourse lies in this final aspect (as we already mentioned in the Introduction with a nod to a critical comparison between Pearl Jam and Radiohead), in the radically different, if not unique, approach Radiohead has adopted in facing these challenges, able to absorb them and transfigure them through its aesthetics. Due to the band's lucid and complex relationship with technology (and its emancipatory aspects, without however hiding the existence also of its oppressive aspects), Radiohead was able to find unexpected and innovative methods of escaping from the risk of a blinding, paralyzing dead end that, according to Fisher's interpretation, marked the musical situation of the period following Cobain's death. This point of view is shared in Alessandro Alfieri's analysis of Radiohead and his observation that what mainly characterizes the English band (mostly musically, of course, but also in terms of the philosophical implications of its music) is

> the role that electronic technology and digital sounds played in the landscape of rock music; the role of synthesizers and computers in pop music has roots in the 1970s, but the use of computer processes and electronic instruments gained a greater level of expressivity able to free itself from simply being self-aggrandizing productions of a technological and science fiction approach. [...] Synthetic experimentation is absorbed by Radiohead in a *crucial moment* of its career, which could have determined a *creative asphyxiation* or *parallels* with many other musicians and groups that came to fame in the early 1990s. [...] The *intuition* that would determine Radiohead's career [was] electronic experimentation and artistic exploration as a possibility to *reintroduce itself in an irreducibly specific way*: for Radiohead, experimentation became an opportunity to avoid *succumbing to self-destructive nihilism.* [...] Radiohead, *different from any band from recent decades – and comparable to just a handful of other bands in the history of rock –* is able to create an aesthetics and an imaginary freed from the trap of becoming retro and dramatic essentialism, becoming a *source of inspiration* for many rock bands that would follow. To complete this transition, the band from Oxfordshire abandoned minimalism and veered towards a certain scru-

---

73   Alfieri 2019, p. 25 (emphasis added).

pulousness in the compositions and an attention to sound and the installations of the live performances that [...] maintain the *spontaneity* of the band's origins alongside an evolution that saw as its major source the *use of technology*.[74]

As we have already seen, according to Adorno (who, as we mentioned earlier, thought that the paths of «serious» and «light» music were never again forced together after Mozart's *Magic Flute*, to the point that they should be understood as separated by an abyss),[75] in our age the secret law of development of the history of music must lies in the search for the «flight from the banal.[76]» If this philosophical-musical conception is useful in explaining at least the main adventures of «serious music» of recent centuries, and in particular of avant-garde music, one is also tempted to apply it to some of the many paths taken (sometimes successfully, other times less so) by what we may call «radical pop music.» In fact, as has been observed by Giacomo Fronzi,

> in the second half of the 20th century an unprecedented, almost curious situation arose, in that radical music, committed to recovering (or creating *ex novo*) a relationship with the audience, came close to being popular, and popular music, especially rock, tended to become increasingly radical. [...] Like serious music, some examples of popular music are able to conquer the more advanced stage of their musical material, being aware of the techniques and instruments at their disposal, and attempting to escape their fate as merchandise. The reference to «radical» pop music also makes it still clearer that the relationship between the contemporary musical world and the audience at this time is a complex one.[77]

The notion of «radical pop music» is undoubtedly fitting and veritably capable to also include Radiohead's music (or, at least, all post-*The Bends* Radiohead), keeping in mind how, at the same

---

74   Alfieri 2019, pp. 61, 63, 65, 68 (emphasis added).
75   «*The Magic Flute*, in which the utopia of the Enlightenment and the pleasure of a light opera comic song precisely coincide, is a moment by itself. After *The Magic Flute* it was never again possible to force serious and light music together» (Adorno 2001, p. 32).
76   Adorno 2001, p. 34.
77   Fronzi 2017, pp. 109-110.

time, Radiohead's avant-garde and radical development is based *first and foremost* on the band's extremely original attempt at fusing technology and expression (which we have condensed into the word «soul»); *secondly*, this development rests on the fact that the group never suffocated or censured, in virtue of the necessities of experimental radicalism as the antidote to the power of the banal, a legitimate dimension of aesthetic gratification, enjoyableness and singability. Therefore, even from this point of view Radiohead's music proves to be philosophical fruitful and stimulating, to the extent that, keeping in mind the example offered by Thom Yorke, Jonny Greenwood, Colin Greenwood, Ed O'Brien and Philip Selway, it is quite easy to recognize the validity of some observations on popular art (and, more specifically, rock music) of Richard Shusterman, when he explains that

> [t]he strongest and most urgent reason for defending popular art is that it provides us (even us intellectuals) with too much aesthetic satisfaction to accept its wholesale denunciation as debased, dehumanizing, and aesthetically illegitimate. To condemn it as fit only for the barbaric taste and dull wit of the unenlightened, manipulated masses is to divide us not only against the rest of our community but against ourselves. [...] [P]opular art not only can satisfy the most important standards of our aesthetic tradition, but also has the power to enrich and refashion our traditional concept of the aesthetic, so as to liberate it more fully from its alienating association with class privilege, socio-political inaction, and the ascetic denial of life. [...] Rock songs are typically enjoyed through moving, dancing, and singing along with the music, often with such vigorous efforts that we break a sweat and eventually exhaust ourselves. [...] Clearly, on the somatic level, there is much more effortful activity in the appreciation of rock than in that of high-brow music [...]. The term «funky,» used to characterize and commend many rock songs, derives from an African word meaning «positive sweat» and is expressive of an African aesthetic of vigorously active and communally impassioned engagement rather than dispassionate judgmental remoteness. [...] Popular arts like rock thus suggest a radically revised aesthetic with a joyous return of the somatic dimension.[78]

---

78   Shusterman 2000, pp. 170, 173, 184.

As the musicologists Carl Dahlhaus and Hans H. Eggebrecht once noted, «the critical debate on the dichotomy» between so-called «serious» and «light» music has (unfortunately) often appeared, throughout the 20th century, as a sort of «skewed, lopsided, distorted dialogue.[79]» If this is so, then the example of a band like Radiohead – with its extraordinary musical evolution, which can be articulated in different phases of development, and its musical aesthetics, rich with its stimulating sound and its remarkable philosophical implications – offers an irresistible invitation to go beyond this never-ending argument and to open our ears and our minds, so that we are always ready to embark on «new adventures in hi-fi.[80]»

---

79   Dahlhaus and Eggebrecht 1985, p. 92.
80   In conclusion, this is a clear reference to the title of the tenth studio album of R.E.M., one of Thom Yorke's favorite bands.

BIBLIOGRAPHY

Adorno, Th. W. (1976). *Introduction to the Sociology of Music*, The Seabury Press, New York.

Adorno, Th. W. (1977a). «The Actuality of Philosophy,» *Telos*, 31, pp. 113-133.

Adorno, Th. W. (1977b). «Music and Technique,» *Telos*, 32, pp. 79-94.

Adorno, Th. W. (1988). «The Aging of the New Music,» *Telos*, 77, pp. 95-116.

Adorno, Th. W. (1993). *Hegel. Three Studies*, The MIT Press, Cambridge (MA)-London.

Adorno, Th. W. (1996). *Probleme der Moralphilosophie*, Suhrkamp, Frankfurt a.M.

Adorno, Th. W. (1997). *Prisms*, The MIT Press, Cambridge (MA).

Adorno, Th. W. (2000). *Metaphysics: Concept and Problems*, Stanford University Press, Stanford (CA).

Adorno, Th. W. (2001). *The Culture Industry: Selected Essays on Mass Culture*, Routledge, London.

Adorno, Th. W. (2002a). *Aesthetic Theory*, Continuum, London-New York.

Adorno, Th. W. (2002b). *Essays on Music*, The University of California Press, Berkeley (CA).

Adorno, Th. W. (2004). *Negative Dialectics*, Routledge, London-New York.

Adorno, Th. W. (2005). *Minima Moralia: Reflections on a Damaged Life*, Verso, London-New York.

Adorno, Th. W. (2009). *Current of Music: Elements of a Radio Theory*, Polity Press, Cambridge-Malden (MA).

Adorno, Th. W. (2016). *Philosophy of Modern Music*, Bloomsbury, London-New York.

Adorno, Th. W. and Benjamin, W. (1999). *The Complete Correspondence: 1928-1940*, Harvard University Press, Cambridge (MA).

Alfieri, A. (2019). *Rocksofia. Filosofia dell'hard rock nel passaggio di millennio*, il melangolo, Genova.

Alighieri, D. (1952). *The Divine Comedy of Dante Alighieri*, Encyclopaedia Britannica, Chicago-London-Toronto-Geneva.

Alighieri, D. (1982). *The Divine Comedy* (with 136 illustrations of Gustave Doré), Chartwell Books, Inc., Secaucus (NJ).

Anders, G. (1956). *Die Antiquiertheit des Menschen: Über die Seele im Zeitalter der zweiten industriellen Revolution*, Beck, München.

Arendt, H. (1958), *The Human Condition*, Doubleday, Garden City (NY).

Asquini, A. (2011). «Review of Radiohead, *The King of Limbs*,» *Ondarock*, 23 February 2011 (available at: https://www.ondarock.it/recensioni/2011_Radiohead.htm).

Banti, A.M. (2017). *Wonderland. La cultura di massa da Walt Disney ai Pink Floyd*, Laterza, Roma-Bari.

Benjamin, W. (2008). *The Work of Art in the Age of Its Technological Reproducibility, and Other Writings, on Media*, Harvard University Press, Cambridge (MA)-London.

Bertinetto, A. (2022). *Aesthetics of Improvisation*, Brill, Leiden-Boston.

Bertoncelli, R. (1999). *Storia leggendaria della musica rock*, Giunti, Firenze.

Burt, S. (2009). «The Impossible Utopias in *Hail to the Thief*,» in B.W. Forbes and G.A. Reisch (ed.), *Radiohead and Philosophy: Fitter, Happier, More Deductive*, Open Court, Chicago-La Salle, pp. 89-93.

Castelli, L. (2022). *Nel labirinto. Thom Yorke. Storie, mito e musica*, Sperling & Kupfer, Milano.

Chiais, E. (2020). «From the Bronx to the Boutiques: The Rise of Street Style in the Fashion Industry,» *The Culture, Fashion, and Society Notebook*, pp. 75-97.

Chitussi, B. (2010). *Immagine e mito. Un carteggio tra Benjamin e Adorno*, Mimesis, Milano-Udine.

Cook, D. (2011). *Adorno on Nature*, Acumen, Durham.

Dahlhaus, C. and Eggebrecht, H. H. (1985). *Was ist der Musik?*, Heinrichshofen's Verlag, Wilhelmshaven.

Doheny, J. (2002). *Radiohead. Karma Police: The Stories behind Every Song*, Carlton, London.

Draper, B. (2004). «Chipping Away: Briad Draper talks to Thom Yorke,» *Third Way*, 27, 10, pp. 16-21 (available at: https://highprofiles.info/interview/thom-yorke).

Fabbri, F. (2008). *Around the Clock. Una breve storia della popular music*, UTET, Torino.

Ferdori, D. and Marino, S. (ed.) (2013). *Filosofia e Popular Music. Da Zappa ai Beach Boys, dai Doors agli U2*, Mimesis, Milano-Udine.

Ferretti, G.L. and Zamboni, M. (1998). *Il libretto rozzo dei CCCP e CSI. Tutti i testi e scritti inediti*, Giunti, Firenze.

Fiorelli, L. (2009). «Fitter Happier Rolling a Large Rock Up a Hill,» in B.W. Forbes and G.A. Reisch (ed.), *Radiohead and Philosophy: Fitter, Happier, More Deductive*, Open Court, Chicago-La Salle, pp. 123-126.

Fischer-Lichte, E. (2008). *The Transformative Power of Performance: A New Aesthetics*, Routledge, London-New York.

Fisher, J.A. (2011). «Popular Music,» in Th. Gracyk and A. Kania (ed.), *The Routledge Companion to Philosophy and Music*, Routledge, London, pp. 405-415.

Fisher, M. (2009). *Capitalist Realism: Is There No Alternative?*, Zero Books, Alresford.

Fisher, M. (2014). *Ghosts of my Life: Writings on Depression, Hauntology and Lost Futures*, Zero Books, Alresford.

Footman, T. 2007. *Radiohead. Welcome to the Machine:* OK Computer *and the Death of the Classic Album*, Chrome Dreams, New Malden.

Forbes, B.W. (2009). «Where Power Ends and Violence Begins,» in B.W. Forbes and G.A. Reisch (ed.), *Radiohead and Philosophy: Fitter, Happier, More Deductive*, Open Court, Chicago-La Salle, pp. 94-98.

Forbes, B.W. and Reisch, G.A. (ed.) (2009). *Radiohead and Philosophy: Fitter, Happier, More Deductive*, Open Court, Chicago-La Salle.

Franchi, G. (2009). *Radiohead. A Kid. Testi commentati*, Arcana, Roma.

Friberg, C. (2024). «Delusions about the Human in the Anthropocene,» *Nordicum-Mediterraneum: Icelandic E-Journal of Nordic and Mediterranean Studies*, 19, 2 (available at: https://nome.unak.is /wordpress/volume-19-no-2-2024/new-article-double-blind-peer-review-volume-18-no-3-2024/delusions-about-the-human -in-the-anthropocene).

Frickle, D. (2003). «Bitter Prophet: Thom Yorke on *Hail to the Thief*,» *Rolling Stone*, 26 June 2003 (available at: https://www.rollingstone.com/music/music-news/bitter-prophet-thom-yorke-on-hail-to-the-thief-87869).

Fronzi, G. (2017). *Philosophical Considerations on Contemporary Music: Sounding Constellations*, Cambridge Scholars Publishing, Newcastle.

Fronzi, G. (2021). *Percorsi musicali del Novecento. Storie, personaggi, poetiche da Schönberg a Sciarrino*, Carocci, Roma.

Früchtl, J. (2019). «*Message in a Bottle*: Adornos kritische Theorie und die Popkultur,» lecture at the international conference *Adorno and the Media* (13-14 December 2019), held at the Staatliche Hochschule für Gestaltung in Karlsruhe (available at: https://www.hfg-karlsruhe.de/en/aktuelles/call-for-papers-adorno-und-die-medien).

Gadamer, H.-G. (1986). *The Relevance of the Beautiful and Other Essays*, Cambridge University Press, Cambridge.

Gandesha, S. and Hartle, J. F. (ed.) (2017). *Aesthetic Marx*, Bloomsbury, London-New York.

Gandesha, S., Hartle, J. F. and Marino, S. (ed.) (2021). *The «Aging» of Adorno's Aesthetic Theory: Fifty Years Later*, Mimesis International, Milano-Udine.

Goehr, L. (1992). *The Imaginary Museum of Musical Works: An Essay in the Philosophy of Music*, Clarendon Press, Oxford.

Gracyk, Th. (1996). *Rhythm and Noise: An Aesthetics of Rock*, Duke University Press, Durham.

Gracyk, Th. (2007). *Listening to Popular Music: Or, How I Learned to Stop Worrying and Love Led Zeppelin*, The University of Michigan Press, Ann Arbor.

Greenberg, C. (1957). «Avant-Garde and Kitsch,» in B. Rosenberg and D. Manning White (ed.), *Mass Culture: The Popular Arts in America*, The Free Press, Glencoe (Ill.), pp. 98-110

Heidegger, M. (1977). *The Question Concerning Technology and Other Essays*, Harper & Row, New York.

Heidegger, M. (1996). *Being and Time*, State University of New York Press, Albany (NY).

Horkheimer, M. (1985). «Philosophie als Kulturkritik,» in *Gesammelte Schriften. Band 7: Vorträge und Aufzeichnungen 1949-1973*, Fischer Verlag, Frankfurt a.M., pp. 81-103.

Horkheimer, M. (2004). *Eclipse of Reason*, Continuum, London-New York.

Horkheimer, M. and Adorno, Th. W. (2002). *Dialectic of Enlightenment: Philosophical Fragments*, Stanford University Press, Stanford (CA).

Hyden, S. (2021). *This Isn't Happening: Radiohead's* Kid A *and the Beginning of the 21*[st] *Century*, Hachette Books, New York.

Inwood, M. (1999). *A Heidegger Dictionary*, Blackwell, Oxford-Maiden (MA).

Kramer, S. (2021). «"They Can Buy, But Can't Put On My Clothes": Pearl Jam, Grunge, and Subcultural Authenticity in a Postmodern Fashion Climate,» in S. Marino and A. Schembari (ed.), *Pearl Jam and Philosophy*, Bloomsbury, London-New York, pp. 139-164.

KRT (2003). «Radiohead Set to Steal the Show Again,» *The Age*, 4 June 2003 (available at: https://www.theage.com.au/entertainment/music/ Radiohead-set-to-steal-the-show-again-20030604-gdvtmk.html).

Lee, J. (2009). «Evil and Politics in *Hail to the Thief*,» in B.W. Forbes and G.A. Reisch (ed.), *Radiohead and Philosophy: Fitter, Happier, More Deductive*, Open Court, Chicago-La Salle, pp. 99-102.

Leight, E. (2016). «Dr. Rachel Owen, Former Partner of Thom Yorke, Dead at Age 48,» *Rolling Stone*, 20 December 2016 (available at: https:// www.rollingstone.com/music/music-news/dr-rachel-owen-former-partner-of-thom-yorke-dead-at-age-48-106092).

Letts Tatom, M. (2010). *Radiohead and the Resistant Concept Album: How to Disappear Completely*, Indiana University Press, Bloomington (IN).

Lin, M. (2018). *Kid A*, Bloomsbury, London.

Lipovetsky, G. and Serroy, J. (2016). *L'esthétisation du monde. Vivre à l'âge du capitalisme artiste*, Gallimard, Paris.

Lougheed, D. (2009). «Nietzsche, Nihilism, and *Hail to the Thief*,» in B.W. Forbes and G.A. Reisch (ed.), *Radiohead and Philosophy: Fitter, Happier, More Deductive*, Open Court, Chicago-La Salle, pp. 79-82.

Macdonald, D. (1962). «Masscult & Midcult,» in *Against The American Grain: Essays on The Effects of Mass Culture*, Random House, New York, pp. 3-77.

Marcuse, H. (2007). «The Affirmative Character of Culture,» in *Art and Liberation. Collected Papers of Herbert Marcuse, Volume 4*, Routledge, London-New York.

Marino, S. (2014). *La filosofia di Frank Zappa. Un'interpretazione adorniana*, Mimesis, Milano-Udine.

Marino, S. (2015). «Gadamer and McDowell on Second Nature, World/ Environment, and Language,» in *Aesthetics, Metaphysics, Language: Essays on Heidegger and Gadamer*, Cambridge Scholars Publishing, Newcastle, pp. 5-47.

Marino, S. (2019). *Le verità del non-vero. Tre studi su Adorno, teoria critica ed estetica*, Mimesis, Milano-Udine.

Marino, S. (2020). «Second-Nature Aesthetics: On the Very Idea of Human Environment,» *Aesthetica Preprint*, 114, pp. 113-135.

Marino, S. (2021a). «Critical Theory vs. Philosophical Anthropology on Radio and TV: Some Remarks on Adorno and Gehlen,» *Studi di estetica*, 19, 1, pp. 197-219.

Marino, S. (2021b). *Verità e non-verità del popular. Saggio su Adorno, dimensione estetica e critica della società*, Mimesis, Milano-Udine.

Marino, S. (2022). «Fine dell'arte,» *Nuova Informazione Bibliografica*, 19, 4, pp. 603-626.

Marino, S. and Schembari, A. (ed.) (2021). *Pearl Jam and Philosophy*, Bloomsbury, London-New York.

Mattioli, V. (2018). *La funzione Fisher*, preface to M. Fisher, *Realismo capitalista*, Nero, Roma, pp. 7-20.

Maurizi, M. (2018). *La vendetta di Dioniso. La musica contemporanea da Schönberg ai Nirvana*, Jaca Book, Milano.

Maurizi, M. (2019). «The Unbearable Lightness of Music? Adorno's Critique of the Music Industry,» in C. J. Campbell, S. Gandesha and S. Marino (ed.), *Adorno and Popular Music. A Constellation of Perspectives*, Mimesis International, Milano-Udine, pp. 123-148.

Mazzarella, E. (1987). «La *Seinsfrage* come *Kehre* e come *Denkweg*,» introduction to M. Heidegger, *Tempo ed essere*, Guida, Napoli, pp. 9-97.

McLean, C. (2007). «Caught in the Flash,» *The Guardian*, 9 December 2007 (available at: https://www.theguardian.com/music/2007/dec/09/popandrock.Radiohead1).

Mecacci, E. (2011). *L'estetica del pop*, Donzelli, Roma.

Mehldau, B. (2005). «Radiohead, Coltrane and Me,» *The Guardian*, 26 September 2005 (available at: https://www.theguardian.com/music/2005/sep/26/popandrock).

Mehldau, B. (2015). *10 Years Solo Live (Booklet)*, 4 CD box, Nonesuch Records.

Melançon, J. (2009). «The Real Politics in Radiohead,» in B.W. Forbes and G.A. Reisch (ed.), *Radiohead and Philosophy: Fitter, Happier, More Deductive*, Open Court, Chicago-La Salle, pp. 83-88.

Melissano, M. (2003). *Le canzoni dei Radiohead*, Editori Riuniti, Roma.

Michaud, Y. 2019. *L'arte allo stato gassoso. Saggio sul trionfo dell'estetica*, Mimesis, Milano-Udine (original edition: *L'Art à l'état gazeux. Essai sur le triomphe de l'esthétique*, Éditions Stock, Paris 2003).

Miller, P. (2013). «Why Steve Reich Was Inspired by the Work of Radiohead's Jonny Greenwood,» *The Herald*, 27 February 2013 (available at:

https://www.heraldscotland.com/life_style/arts_ents/13093828. steve-reich-inspired-work-Radioheads-jonny-greenwood).

Milsky, D. (2009). «Taking the Sting Out of Environmental Virtue Ethics,» in B.W. Forbes and G.A. Reisch (ed.), *Radiohead and Philosophy: Fitter, Happier, More Deductive*, Open Court, Chicago-La Salle, pp. 62-66.

Moore, A.F. (2011) «Rock,» in Th. Gracyk and A. Kania (ed.), *The Routledge Companion to Philosophy and Music*, Routledge, London, pp. 416-425.

Nacci, M. (2000). *Pensare la tecnica. Un secolo di incomprensioni*, Laterza, Roma-Bari.

Newport, C. (2019). *Digital Minimalism: Choosing a Focused Life in a Noisy World*, Penguin Books, New York (ebook version).

Nietzsche, F. (1996). *Human, All Too Human: A Book for Free Spirits*, Cambridge University Press, Cambridge.

Nietzsche, F. (2007). *Ecce Homo: How To Become What You Are*, Oxford University Press, Oxford.

Noë, A. (2015). *Strange Tools: Art and Human Nature*, Hill and Wang, New York.

Oppenheim, M. (2017). «Glastonbury crowd erupts into shouts of "Oh Jeremy Corbyn" after Radiohead condemns "useless politicians",» *The Independent*, 26 June 2017 (available at: https://www.independent.co.uk/arts-entertainment/music/news/glastonbury-2017-radiohead-jeremy-corbyn-song-crowd-useless-politicians-thom-yorke-a7808506.html).

Parapar, C. (2021). «Pearl Jam: Responsible Music or the Tragedy of Culture?,» in S. Marino and A. Schembari (ed.), *Pearl Jam and Philosophy*, Bloomsbury, London-New York, pp. 183-203.

Pattison, L. (2012). «Steve Reich: "It's Beethoven on Mondays and Radiohead on Tuesdays",» *The Guardian*, 30 June 2012 (available at: https://www.theguardian.com/music/2012/jun/30/steve-reich-bloc-weekender).

Petridis, A. (2013). «Steve Reich on Schoenberg, Coltrane and Radiohead,» *The Guardian*, 1 March 2013 (available at: https://www.theguardian.com/music/2013/mar/01/steve-reich-schoenberg-coltrane-Radiohead).

Proust, M. (1981). *Swann's Way. Within a Budding Grove*, vol. 1 of *Remembrance of Things Past*, Random House, New York.

Radiohead (2017). *Radiohead Complete (Images, Lyrics, Chords)*, Faber Music Ltd, London.

Randall, M. (2011). *Exit Music: The Radiohead Story*, Omnibus Press, London.

Rausa, G. (2005). *Dizionario della musica rock*, 2 vols., BUR, Milano.

Reich, S. (2013). «Radio Rewrite» (available at: https://www.nonesuch.com/albums/radio-rewrite).

Rennis, F. (2018). *Politics. La musica angloamericana nell'era di Trump e della Brexit*, Arcana, Roma.

Reynolds, S. (2011). *Retromania: Pop Culture's Addiction to Its Own Past*, Faber and Faber, New York (ebook version).

Rognoni, L. (1966). *Fenomenologia della musica radicale*, Laterza, Bari 1966.

Ross, A. (2007). *The Rest Is Noise: Listening to the Twentieth Century*, Picador, New York.

Ruggenini, M. (2002). «L'essenza della tecnica e il nichilismo,» in F. Volpi (ed.), *Guida a Heidegger*, Laterza, Roma-Bari, pp. 225-264.

Schweppenhäuser, G. (2003). «Das Glück "jenseits des Pedestren" und die Ehre der Fußgänger. Anmerkungen zu Adornos Wahrheitsbegriff,» *Zeitschrift für kritische Theorie*, 9, 17, pp. 27-72.

Shusterman, R. (2000). *Pragmatist Aesthetics: Living Beauty, Rethinking Art*, Rowman & Littlefield: Lanham-Boulder-New York-Oxford.

Simmel, G. (1997). «The Metropolis and Mental Life,» in *Simmel on Culture: Selected Writings*, Sage Publications, London-Thousand Oaks-New Delhi, pp. 174-185.

Solventi, S. (2018). *The Gloaming. I Radiohead e il crepuscolo del rock*, Odoya, Bologna.

Svendsen, L.F. (2006). *Fashion: A Philosophy*, Reaktion Books, London.

Tamm, E. (1990). *Robert Fripp: From King Crimson to Guitar Craft*, Faber & Faber, London.

Tate, J. (2009). «We (Capitalists) Suck Young Blood,» in B.W. Forbes and G.A. Reisch (ed.), *Radiohead and Philosophy: Fitter, Happier, More Deductive*, Open Court, Chicago-La Salle, pp. 67-71.

Thompson, M. (2009). «The Signature of Time in *Pyramid Song*,» in B.W. Forbes and G.A. Reisch (ed.), *Radiohead and Philosophy: Fitter, Happier, More Deductive*, Open Court, Chicago-La Salle, pp. 119-122.

Valagussa, F. (2013). *L'età della morte dell'arte*, il Mulino, Bologna.

Velotti, S. (2005). «Arte,» in G. Carchia and P. D'Angelo (ed.), *Dizionario di estetica*, Laterza, Roma-Bari, pp. 17-21.

Vercellone, F. (2013). *Dopo la morte dell'arte*, il Mulino, Bologna.

Vitta, M. (2012). *Il rifiuto degli dèi. Teoria delle belle arti industriali*, Einaudi, Torino.

Vizzardelli, S. (2007). *Filosofia della musica*, Laterza, Roma-Bari.

Witkin, R. (1998). *Adorno on Music*, Routledge, London-New York.

Witkin, R. (2000). «Why did Adorno "Hate" Jazz?», *Sociological Theory*, 18, 1, pp. 145-170.

Wittkower, D.E. (2009). «Everybody Hates Rainbows,» in B.W. Forbes and G.A. Reisch (ed.), *Radiohead and Philosophy: Fitter, Happier, More Deductive*, Open Court, Chicago-La Salle, pp. 72-76.

Zucco, G. (2016). «*True Love Waits*. L'amore, i Radiohead, ventuno anni dopo,» *Minima & Moralia*, 12 June 2016 (available at: https://www. minimaetmoralia.it/wp/musica/i-Radiohead-ventuno-anni-dopo).

Printed by
Rotomail Italia S.p.A
October 2024